DIFFERENT DISCIPLESHIP

JESUS' SERMON ON THE MOUNT

COMMENTARY, STUDY GUIDE AND PRAYER PROMPT

COMPILED BY HAYES PRESS

Different Discipleship: Jesus' Sermon On The Mount

Published by Hayes Press (**www.hayespress.org**)

The Barn, Flaxlands, Royal Wootton Bassett, Wiltshire, UK SN4 8DY 01793 850598

Book and Cover design by Hayden Press. For information contact: haydenpress2011@gmail.com

ISBN: 9781871126204

Second Edition: December 2015

10 9 8 7 6 5 4 3 2

CONTENTS

ABOUT THE AUTHORS

Chapter One: George Prasher Jnr.

Chapter Two: Alan Toms

Chapter Three: Alan Toms

Chapter Four: Alan Toms

Chapter Five: Alan Toms

Chapter Six: Bob Armstrong

Chapter Seven: Ken Riley

Chapter Eight: Lindsay Prasher

Chapter Nine: Brian Fullarton

Chapter Ten: Ed Neely

Chapter Eleven: Keith Dorricott

Chapter Twelve: John Miller

Chapter Thirteen: Bill McCubbin

1: THE SETTING OF THE SERMON

It was Miles Coverdale, hundreds of years ago, who offered this quaint but valuable advice for the clearer understanding of God's word: "It shall greatly help thee to understand Scripture if thou mark not only what is spoken or written: but of whom: and to whom: with what words: at what time: where: with what intent: with what circumstances: considering what goeth before and what followeth after."

Certainly the wonderful discourse of the Lord Jesus recorded in Matthew 5 to 7 calls for this approach. Few parts of the Bible have attracted greater admiration, even from people who have little understanding of God's Word as a whole. Many who have never experienced the new birth will lift out parts of the Lord's teaching from these chapters as a good rule of life. Notably, they like to quote what they regard as a golden rule: "In everything, do to others what you would have them do to you" (7:12 NIV). But the casual use of a fragment here and there doesn't do justice to the tremendous message of the discourse from the lips of the incomparable Teacher, who spoke with divine authority and wisdom. But before we spend time looking at the detail of Jesus' message, let's take a look at the context of the sermon.

The Relationship to the Age of Law

The age or "dispensation" of the law ran from Moses until Christ. The Lord Jesus was "born under the law" (Galatians 4:4). He acknowledged its continuing authority "till all things be accomplished" (Matthew 5:18). He Himself magnified the law and made it honourable in His own perfect accomplishment of all it required (Isaiah 42:21). He redeemed us from the curse of the law, having become a curse for us (Galatians 3:13). So when He had died and risen again the age of the law drew to a close, to be followed by the present glorious age of grace, ushered in by the outpouring of the Holy Spirit on the Day of Pentecost. From that day forward the word was true: "you are not under law, but under grace" (Romans 6:14 NIV).

It was, then, in the closing years of the age of law that the Lord Jesus gave "the Sermon on the Mount." He was speaking to those under the law, to a Jewish audience in the Palestine of His day. They recognized the Old Testament as God's "living oracles" (Acts 7:38). The Lord firmly upheld them as of divine origin and authority (Matthew 5:17,18) - so much so that to break "one of these least commandments" would result in being called least in the kingdom of heaven; but to do and teach them would bring corresponding honour. Moreover, those who claimed to be the custodians and ideal exponents of that law, the scribes and Pharisees, were said to have fallen short of its requirements (Matthew 5:20).

The whole presentation of the Lord's message on this occasion had regard to Jewish background and spiritual thought. We find glimpses of features so familiar in their experience: the gift brought to the altar (Matthew 5:23); the city of the great King (Matthew 5:35); publicly announced giving to the poor (Matthew 6:2); and hypocrites praying in the streets (Matthew 6:5).

References to the Kingdom of Heaven

These references should also be understood in relation to the outlook of the people to whom the Lord Jesus was speaking. For at that time, the people of Israel where obsessed with the expectation of deliverance from Rome's political yoke through the setting up of Messiah's kingdom. Hadn't Isaiah foretold that "of the increase of His government and of peace there shall be no end, upon the throne of David, and upon His kingdom, to establish it, and to uphold it with judgement and with righteousness ... for ever"? (Isaiah 9:7). Hadn't Daniel in vision seen the glory of the nation's promise Messiah - "and there was given Him dominion, and glory, and a kingdom ... which shall not pass away (Daniel 7:14)?

So Jewish hopes for future glory lay in that promised messianic kingdom, the kingdom of heaven, the rule of heaven through Messiah in this world. The same outlook is seen in Luke 19:11, when the Lord added the parable of the ten servants and their pounds "because they supposed that the kingdom of God was immediately to appear." While even after the Lord's resurrection the disciples seemed to be cherishing this hope when they asked Him, "... will You at this time restore the kingdom to Israel?" (Acts 1:6).

A reference to the kingdom of heaven in Matthew 7:21 seems

to demand this identification with the future kingdom of Messiah. For the following verses refer to a day of accountability and judgement; in that day some will enter the kingdom of heaven and others will be excluded. This agrees with what the Lord said in Matthew 8:11-12. Many Gentiles will share the blessings of the kingdom of heaven with Abraham, Isaac and Jacob, but the "sons of the kingdom", those who by natural birth should have had a place there, will be cast out. To what could this apply if not to the future earthly kingdom of Messiah? It's significant that in the parallel verses in Luke's gospel (Luke 13:28-29) this is referred to as the kingdom of God. So the millennial kingdom of Christ is described in certain contexts both as the kingdom of God and the kingdom of heaven.

Looking at the references to the kingdom of heaven in the Sermon on the Mount, we suggest that each of them refers to that future kingdom - the time of compensation and reward for the poor in spirit and persecuted (Matthew 5:3,10); a sphere of blessing from which the self-righteous and hypocritical will be shut out (Matthew 5:20; 7:21). It would seem that the Lord's hearers would understand His reference to the kingdom of heaven in this sense.

References to Gehenna
Gehenna was the place outside Jerusalem in the Valley of Hinnom where the city's refuse was burned with continuous fire. Figuratively, it represented to the Jewish mind the place of future judgement after this life. This is clear from Mark 9:47 where the entrance for the righteous into the kingdom of God (in this context the future kingdom of Messiah), is contrasted with being cast into hell for judgement. The word Gehenna is again translated "hell" in Luke 12:4-5, confirming that to be cast into

Gehenna means divine punishment after death. The three references in Matthew 5:22, 29-30 are all in a similar sense, pointing to the judgement of God in hell. The Lord was warning that whereas such acts as murder or adultery were acknowledged to merit such judgement, even angry words or impure thoughts springing from the evil motivations of the heart were seriously sinful. These, too, could make a person liable to divine judgement.

Links with the Dispensation of Grace

In some respects, Jesus' teaching in the Sermon on the Mount anticipated the fuller revelation and higher standards of this present age of grace. Paul wrote in Romans 8:3-4: "What the law could not do, in that it was weak through the flesh, God, sending His own Son in the likeness of sinful flesh and as an offering for sin, condemned sin in the flesh: that the ordinance of the law might be fulfilled in us, who walk not after the flesh, but after the Spirit." Jesus was pointing the way in this direction. He showed that more was needed than mere outward compliance with the letter of law. He dealt also with inward motivation. For instance, the commandment not to commit adultery applied not only to the physical act. Adultery may be committed in the heart by looking lustfully at a woman (Matthew 5:28). So He demonstrated that men did not fully keep God's law. Pharisee and scribe might claim to do so, but theirs was a superficial self-righteousness.

Jesus' teaching began to impress on Jewish hearts what became so clear in the new dispensation that "the law was our tutor to bring us unto Christ, that we might be justified by faith" (Galatians 3:24). It shows our failure and essential unrighteousness, and so prepares us to trust alone in Him "who was made unto us wisdom from God, and righteousness and sanctification, and redemption" (1 Corinthians 1:30). Having appreciated this, we may then as Spirit-indwelt believers in Jesus fulfil the requirement of the law, walking "not after the flesh, but after the Spirit."

Besides such preparatory teaching towards great foundation principles of the dispensation of grace, Jesus' ministry in Matthew 5 touches several matters in which higher standards where then to be introduced. His teaching as to marriage (Matthew 5:31-32), the taking of oaths (Matthew 5:33-37), and love for those who ill-treat us (Matthew 5:43-48) were all later confirmed by the Epistles as guidance for His disciples in the present age.

Spanning all Dispensations!

Much of the matchless teaching in this great discourse by Jesus is fundamental to a right attitude before God throughout all ages of His ways with men. The prophet Micah wrote, "He has shown you, O man, what is good; and what does the Lord require of you, but to do justly, to love mercy, and to walk humbly with your God?" In the setting of the Israel of His day, Jesus presented teaching which simply but brilliantly expressed these beauties of spiritual character; truths which are timeless. For hasn't God always honoured such attitudes of heart as described in the beatitudes (Matthew 5:1-12), and the sincerity of secret prayer or secret giving to others (Matthew 6:1-18), and dependence in faith on Him for daily provision (Matthew 6:19-34), and obedience in faith to His word (Matthew 7:24-27)?

Truth for our Time

As further chapters in this book will now deal in greater detail with these three chapters of Matthew's gospel, may our hearts be open to accept the full impact of the Lord's powerful message! For here is truth that is very largely applicable to you and me today. We shall be so much the poorer if it is lost in our own spiritual experience. Although cast in a Jewish mould suited to the occasion when first it was spoken, the whole sermon forms a pattern of healthful teaching to which we also should give our full attention.

2: HAPPY ARE THE POOR AND MOURNING
(MATTHEW 5:1-4)

The Sermon on the Mount was spoken during the early part of Jesus' ministry when He was very popular with the people. In fact, Matthew says great multitudes followed Him from all parts of the country, and when He saw them He went up into the mountain and taught His disciples. So what He had to say was primarily to His followers, although at the end of the sermon the multitudes were astonished at His teaching - evidently they'd been listening.

"Blessed"

"Blessed are the poor in spirit, for theirs is the kingdom of heaven. Blessed are those who mourn, for they shall be comforted. Blessed are the meek, for they shall inherit the earth," and so on. It's arresting to see that the Lord Jesus began His teaching with the word blessed and repeated it nine times over. What does it mean? Happy? Yes, but more than that - at least more than what the world counts as happiness. The world's happiness can be such a fleeting thing. But the happiness that the Lord Jesus gives comes from a settled peace in the heart, and it doesn't depend upon our circumstances at all. God is described in the Bible as the blessed or happy God, and He wants us to be happy too - happy with a deep sense of well-being, happy in the knowledge that our sins are forgiven and we're bound for heaven.

That's where happiness begins. "Blessed is he whose transgression is forgiven, whose sin is covered," wrote king David (Psalm 32:1), and the apostle Paul quotes his words in Romans chapter 4. And when Simon Peter confessed that the Lord Jesus was the Christ, the Son of the living God, Jesus said, "Blessed are you, Simon Bar-Jonah! For flesh and blood has not revealed this to you, but my Father who is in heaven" (Matthew 16:16-17). That's where happiness begins for any person, when he understands that Jesus is the Son of God, and for his sins and for his salvation He went to Calvary and died. The gospel Paul preached was in two parts, repentance toward God, and that comes when we are convinced of the seriousness of our sin, and faith toward our Lord Jesus Christ, and that happens when we discover, as Peter did, that He is the Son of the living God.

One of the happiest persons I ever met was a little Chinese lady we called Aunty Hannah. She came into my life when I first went to Burma. I thank God for Aunty Hannah and what I learned from her. "Having nothing and yet possessing all things" just described her. She was so poor she could literally pack all her treasures in one small bag and carry them over her shoulder. But she was radiant with the joy of Christ and she used to spend a lot of her time visiting her many Chinese friends and telling them all about Him. Certainly she was living proof that happiness doesn't depend on what you possess, nor upon the circumstances of your life. It's a deeper thing than that. It begins when we accept Christ as our own Saviour, and it grows as we go on to acknowledge Him as Lord.

"Blessed are the poor in spirit"

"Blessed are the poor in spirit, for theirs is the kingdom of heaven." With these impressive words, Jesus began His Sermon on the Mount. Showing us the way to real happiness and leaving us in no doubt whatever that this is what He desires for us so deeply, that we should enjoy this happiness in our lives.

I suppose that's what most people in the world are searching for. If we took a consensus of what people are wanting above anything else, I'm sure happiness would be very high on the list. Men and women seek it in different ways of course - in pleasure and sport, in sex, in politics, sometimes in religion. But are they finding it? They're not, are they? A simple glance through our daily newspaper convinces us of that. They're trying so hard and failing so miserably. The real happiness that lasts, that contentment of spirit which affects a person's whole life is evading them. No, the world hasn't found it, hard as it has tried.

That's why I'm so thankful for the privilege of sharing with you these words the Lord Jesus spoke, for I'm convinced with all my heart they're the answer to the deepest need. Take time to think seriously with me about it, please, and when you've found it yourself, pass it on urgently to others, for time is running out and the message Jesus spoke must be passed around the world.

"Blessed are the poor in spirit," He said, "for theirs is the kingdom of heaven". In other words, that's how we enter the kingdom of heaven and enjoy its lasting happiness. It's not by anything we do, nor by any gifts that we bring. It's an attitude of heart. Blessed are the poor in spirit - what exactly did Jesus mean by that? Certainly it's the very opposite of what the world is advancing. If you want to get ahead believe in yourself, the world says. Self-confidence, self-expression, self-reliance, these are the things our young are learning in schools and colleges. But Jesus said - and His words are undying and their truth lasts for all time - "Blessed are the poor in spirit".

What did He mean? There's a verse in Isaiah 66 which I believe sums it up. God says, "This is the man to whom I will look, he that is humble and contrite in spirit, and trembles at My word". You remember Gideon? He was a young man when God told him He was going to use him to save Israel from their enemies. His reaction is interesting. He said, "My clan is the weakest in Manasseh, and I am the least in my family". That was poverty of spirit, wasn't it? He had small thoughts about himself. To such a man God looked. He was the man God chose to use. Or think of Simon Peter. He had plenty of self-confidence naturally, but when he came to know Jesus he fell at His knees and said, "Depart from me, for I am a sinful man, O Lord" (Luke 5:8). But the Lord didn't depart from him. Not at all. This was the very man He could use, a man who in His presence felt his own unworthiness.

And I believe that leads us right into the secret, if you can call it that, of how we become poor in spirit. The more we get acquainted with God through His Word, the less we shall think of ourselves. The more we learn of Christ, the more He will increase in our estimation, and we shall decrease. And I believe that's what He meant when He said, "Blessed are the poor in spirit, for theirs is the kingdom of heaven". So "Fix your eyes upon Jesus, look full in His glorious face, And the things of earth will grow strangely dim in the light of His glory and grace".

"Blessed are those who mourn"

In the 53rd chapter of Isaiah, Jesus is described as a Man of sorrows and acquainted with grief. It's interesting we never read of Him laughing, but we do read a few times about Him shedding tears. That doesn't mean He wasn't happy, of course. He was, sublimely so. In His parting message to His disciples He said, "These things I have spoken to you, that My joy may be in you, and that your joy may be full" (John 15:11). Like the apostle Paul, He was "sorrowful yet always rejoicing", and I believe that just opens up to us the meaning of the second beatitude: "Blessed are those who mourn, for they shall be comforted".

There may well be a word of comfort here for someone who mourns the loss of a loved one. God has a wonderful way of bringing blessing out of seeming tragedy. The Father of mercies and God of all comfort will comfort your heart in a very special way. But it will not take away from your comfort, I'm sure, if I remind you that Jesus had far more than that in mind when He spoke these words. "Blessed are those who mourn, for they shall be comforted". He was a mourner Himself. He groaned at the grave of Lazarus. "Jesus wept", is the terse way the gospel writer records it. But why? It couldn't have been because His friend Lazarus had died, for in a few minutes He was going to raise him from the dead. Nor was it only in sympathy with the sorrowing sisters, although He was undoubtedly touched by their sorrow. No, there's a deeper reason. The scripture says, "He was deeply moved in spirit and troubled". It was the effect of sin and its fearful results which troubled Him so deeply. That's why He mourned and wept.

The world laughs at sin, but God doesn't. He loathes it. On

every page of His Word He calls on us to take account of the seriousness of sin. The wages of sin is death, the Bible says, and to pay its awful wages, and to free us from its power, God gave His Son in death at Calvary. That is what sin cost God. Let us never forget that. Woodrow Wilson was one of America's God-fearing presidents. He was reputed to be a man of few words. One day when he returned from church his wife asked, "What was the preacher's message today?" "Sin," he replied. "But what did he say about it?" she queried. "He was against it," said the president.

God is against sin. Men laugh about it, but God doesn't. They call it by other names. They cover it up to try and forget its seriousness. "Let us eat, drink and be merry," they say. That's a very common philosophy of life the world's prescription for happiness, but it doesn't last. Hear what Jesus said, "Blessed are those who mourn, for they shall be comforted". That's the way to real happiness. When we mourn over sin, that brings us to repentance and draws us back to God for forgiveness and cleansing. And there's no joy to be compared with the joy of sins forgiven. Let us make known the message that Jesus spoke. Never was it needed more urgently than today. "Blessed are those who mourn, for they shall be comforted".

SUGGESTED PRAYER FOCUS

- For a humble and contrite spirit, with a correct view of self and others.
- For a deep respect for, and fear of, the Word of God.
- For a sense of mourning for personal and global sin.
- For those in this world who have reason to mourn, that they will be comforted.

STUDY QUESTIONS

1. What caught your eye in this chapter for further thought and exploration?

2. Does being poor in spirit involve being miserable and downcast all the time?

3. Read Isaiah 6:5 and Luke 5:8 – are these examples of being "poor in spirit"? If so, what caused them?

4. See Philippians 2:3. Is there a danger of taking 'pride in our humility'? How can we guard against that?

5. Read Romans 8:31 and Philippians 4:13 – how do these verses help to balance our own sense of poverty?

6. See James 4:6 – what else are the poor in spirit promised and for what purpose or reason?

7. Read 2 Corinthians 7:10 – what is the difference between godly sorrow and worldly sorrow?

8. Read Numbers 20:29, Genesis 50:3 and Genesis 50:10. Each mourning had a fixed period – does/should the mourning of a Christian ever come to an end in this life?

9. Read Isaiah 61:1-3 – what was the mourning about here in context, and also prophetically (as Jesus speaking)? Is there an application for us today, or the future?

10. Read Revelation 21:4 – can you grasp what a place without tears or mourning will be like?

STUDY NOTES

3: HAPPY ARE THE MEEK, HUNGRY AND MERCIFUL
(MATTHEW 5:5-7)

"Blessed are the meek"

There is a great deal of confusion about the subject of meekness. Many people are not clear exactly what it means. The Bible says the man Moses was very meek, in fact, the meekest man in all the earth. And it makes that comment at the time when his sister and brother spoke against him because of his wife. Their complaint was completely unfounded and it must have been very hard for Moses to bear. But he didn't attempt to justify himself. There was nothing in him which rose in self-defence. He was content to leave it with God. That was meekness. There is certainly no thought of weakness in it. On the contrary, it is evidence of great spiritual strength.

When Jesus came to live on earth, He said, "I am meek and lowly in heart" (Revised Version). He showed us meekness in perfection. There was no thought of self in Him at all. "When He was reviled, He did not revile in return; when He suffered, He did not threaten; but He trusted to Him who judges justly" (1 Peter 2:23). He must have felt keenly the pain of the scourging and beating, for He was a Man like ourselves. And even more deeply He felt the cruelty and mockery that were hurled at Him. But it produced no resentment in His heart. There was nothing within which rose up in self-defence, or even in self-pity. That was meekness in perfection. And Jesus said, "Blessed are the meek." This is the way to real blessing, to the sort of happiness which God loves to give.

But the reward of the meek is "they shall inherit the earth." How and when we ask? I suppose there's a sense in which they inherit it now, if you take the apostle Paul as an example. "I have all things, and abound," he says (Philippians 4:18 RV). "There is great gain in godliness with contentment" (1 Timothy 6:6). There's no doubt about that, and those who have learned that secret would not wish to change places with anyone else. But I think Jesus was speaking primarily of a future day when he comes to reign, and those who have taken their part in suffering with Him now will reign with Him then. "Do you not know that the saints will judge the world?" asked the apostle Paul of the Corinthians (1 Corinthians 6:2). They ought to have known, but from the way they were behaving I think they had forgotten. Let us not forget. But let Christ's word come right into our hearts today. "Blessed are the meek, for they shall inherit the earth."

The Jewish leaders of Christ's day were expecting Him to seize the reins of government and set up His kingdom and reign as king. But it didn't work that way. He was coming to reign, but not then. The way to the throne was via the cross. Meek and lowly and riding upon a donkey, He came into the capital city to die. And He asks us to follow where He has led the way. The world around us thinks so differently. They think in terms of strength and aggressiveness. That's the world's idea of conquest. But the Man of Calvary, meek and lowly in heart, is still calling us His way, the way of real happiness. "Blessed are the meek, for they shall inherit the earth."

"Blessed are those who hunger and thirst"

Consider the next blessing that Jesus pronounced in His Sermon on the Mount. "Blessed are those who hunger and thirst for righteousness, for they shall be satisfied." Notice it is not those who hunger and thirst for happiness there are plenty of people like that, and they're never satisfied. But those who hunger and thirst for righteousness, these are the ones who are satisfied, and that satisfaction brings real happiness. Jesus said so, and many people the world over are proving His words true.

God speaks about righteousness in two different ways. There is the righteousness which is ours in Christ. It belongs to all who are born again. You remember the apostle Paul says at the end of 2 Corinthians 5, "For our sake He (God) made Him (Jesus) to be sin who knew no sin, so that in Him we might become the righteousness of God." In that sense, God sees all who believe as righteous in Christ. Then there is the righteousness we show in our actions because we are born again. "If you know that He is righteous, you may be sure that every one who does right is born of Him" the apostle John says (1 John 2:29). The first has to do with our justification. God counts us righteous in Christ. The second affects our sanctification which here is a daily experience. "Yield your members to righteousness for sanctification," says Paul in Romans 6:19. In other words we use our bodies to live holy lives.

Righteousness! That is God's standard of what is right. The world cares nothing about it, and the world is not a happy place. Moral standards are crumbling all around us. Men have set aside God's standards but with disastrous results in family life, and with an alarming increase in violence and robbery. Many thoughtful people are wondering what sort of a world our children are being born into. If only men and nations would heed the words of Jesus they would find the happiness and contentment they are so desperately seeking. "Blessed are those who hunger and thirst for righteousness, for they shall be satisfied." These are the happy people.

I'll never forget one of our Chinese friends who lived in Rangoon in Burma. His conversion was very real to him and he just fell in love with the Lord and with his Bible. He was like the blessed man of Psalm 1 who meditated in God's law night and day. No wonder he made such rapid progress spiritually. Everything he read in his Bible he related to his own life. As far as he was concerned all God's commandments were to be obeyed. He almost literally hungered and thirsted after righteousness, and you couldn't have wished for a happier or more contented man.

It's an interesting expression that Jesus uses, for a hungry man just grows more hungry and a thirsty man more thirsty until he is satisfied. And then appetite repeats the process all over again, for hunger and thirst return, and increase, until once again they're satisfied. "As a hart longs for flowing streams, so longs my soul for Thee, O God. My soul thirsts for God, for the living God." "But that's not my experience," you may say. "I don't have that sort of longing after God. I only wish I had." Ah! Christian, it will come, if you get to your Bible. Spend time on your knees each day, asking God to speak to you out of His Word, and you will find your appetite beginning to grow. The more you read and meditate, the more you'll enjoy it, until you are hungering and thirsting for more. The only condition is that you obey what God says, for that is where the righteousness comes in. And then you will understand what Job meant when he said, "I have treasured up the words of His mouth more than my necessary food" (Job 23:12 RV).

"Blessed are the merciful"

One of the highlights of our service for the Lord in Burma was a weekly visit to the local jail. The authorities gave us permission to have a Bible reading with as many of the men as wished to come, and great times they were. The message was so new to most of them. You could see the surprise registering on their faces as the story unfolded. That there was a God in heaven who loved them despite their sin was something wonderful. And to lift them out of it and give them power over it, sending His Son to die, was more wonderful still. Week after week God gave power to His Word, and we marvelled to see it going deep into the hearts of these rough men. In some it worked conviction of sin, and turned them to Christ for salvation.

One of the first to be saved was a college graduate, in for murder. He was naturally quick-tempered and had given the warders a hard time. So when he came to Christ everybody saw the change. Standing up one day in front of the other men he gave his testimony, and we saw the tears trickling down the faces of some of those hardened criminals. "I thought there was no hope for me," he said, "but when I heard of God's love in sending His Son, it dawned on me there was mercy even for me!" How true! There is no limit to His mercy. "God who is rich in mercy, out of the great love with which He loved us, even when we were dead through our trespasses, made us alive with Christ." It has been said that God's grace reaches men in their sin, and His mercy reaches them in their misery. It is God's pity in action, reaching down for our help. "When the kindness of God our Saviour, and His love toward man appeared ... according to His mercy He saved us" (Titus 3:4-5 RV).

Has the mercy of God reached you? If so, then God expects you to show mercy to others. "Blessed are the merciful, for they shall obtain mercy," Jesus said. The good Samaritan showed it the day he met the man dying by the roadside. The priest and the Levite passed by on the other side. But the Samaritan concerned himself with his fellow-traveller's need, and did all in his power to help him. When he had brought him safely to the inn and made provision for him to be well cared for, he went on his way with a glad heart. How do I know that? Because Jesus said, "Blessed are the merciful." There's no happiness to be compared with this. The world seeks its happiness by getting. Jesus said it comes by giving. He told of the servant who owed his master ten thousand talents and because he could not pay his master had mercy on him and forgave him the whole debt. And then he went out and laid hands on one of his fellow-servants who owed him a trivial amount in comparison, and threw him into prison until he paid up. His master was very angry and said "I forgave you all that debt because you besought me; and should not you have had mercy on your fellow-servant, as I had mercy on you?" (Matthew 18:32-33).

Of course he should! And Jesus added this solemn lesson for us all, that we must forgive one another from the heart. Notice that. It must be a heart matter. Not just from our lips but genuinely from our hearts. For if we don't there is the solemn possibility that we shall not be forgiven either. May Jesus' message go deep into our hearts: "Blessed (happy) are the merciful, for they shall obtain mercy.

SUGGESTED PRAYER FOCUS

- For a recurring hunger and thirst for God and his things.
- For help to be "content to fill a little space, if Christ be glorified."
- For the ability to think and act mercifully in a merciless world.

STUDY QUESTIONS

1. Read James 1:21 and Acts 26:14. When God is speaking to us through His Word, what things do we find the hardest to meekly accept – and why?

2. Read James 3:13. What is the 'meekness of wisdom' and how is this displayed in our good works?

3. Read 1 Peter 3:15. Witnessing can often lead to a debating contest or even outright argument – how can we avoid this through being meek, yet still stand firm for the truth?

4. In who or what do we find the righteousness we should be hungering and thirsting for? (See Jeremiah 23:6, 1 John 2:1, Romans 14:17)

5. Read Isaiah 55:2 and Jeremiah 2:12-13. What alternative diets to righteousness are the most tempting today?

6. What should we do if we don't feel hungry or thirsty for righteousness right now?

7. When we become filled with righteousness, what things will happens next? See, for example, Matthew 5:16.

8. Where does our capacity to show mercy come from?

9. Read Matthew 9:10-3. Aren't sacrifices a good thing? Why is mercy more important? (Clue: see Hosea 6:6)

10. How did the "Good Samaritan" in Luke 10 demonstrate mercy?

11. Does our showing mercy have limits? For example, not firing incompetent employees or not punishing a law-breaker?

12. Why does Paul stress in Romans 12:8 that we should be merciful with cheerfulness?

<u>STUDY NOTES</u>

4: HAPPY ARE THE PURE, PEACEABLE AND PERSECUTED
(MATTHEW 5:8-12)

"Blessed are the pure in heart"

Have you noticed a progression in the order in which Jesus spoke the beatitudes? Starting with poverty of spirit, a sense of one's own unworthiness, He went on to pronounce a blessing on those who mourn over sin; and thirdly on the meek, those who have no confidence in self. A meek person recognizes self for what it is, that by his own effort he cannot please God. The first three beatitudes highlight our need and then follows the great statement of that need being met, "Blessed are those who hunger and thirst for righteousness, for they shall be satisfied."

Only God can meet the deep need of the human heart, and He meets it absolutely, satisfying us completely. And when the heart is satisfied - flowing out of the blessedness which Christ gives - we become merciful to others, pure in heart, and peace-makers.

Dr. Martyn Lloyd-Jones makes the interesting point that the first three beatitudes correspond to the last three and he links them together in three couplets. The merciful are those who realize their own poverty of spirit, they acknowledge they are nothing in themselves, and that helps them to be merciful to others. And those who are pure in heart have first of all mourned over sin. And the peace-makers are those who are meek in spirit. A person who is not meek is not likely to be very successful in making peace in another person's life.

But think with me, please, about the sixth statement of Jesus: "Blessed are the pure in heart, for they shall see God." We're all going to see Him, of course, every one of us who has believed. That is the great prospect the apostle John holds out to us in his first epistle. "Beloved, we are God's children now," he says, "it does not yet appear what we shall be, but we know that when He appears we shall be like Him, for we shall see Him as He is" (1 John 3:2). There's a wonderful future ahead of us, Christian. We're going to see our Lord Jesus and be like Him. His servants will do Him service and they will see His face (Revelation 22:3-4).

And then John adds, "Everyone who thus hopes in Him purifies himself as He is pure." If the prospect of being like Him then grips our hearts - if this hope is really working in us - we shall want to be like him now. That's what the Lord Jesus was speaking about. "Blessed are the pure in heart, for they shall see God." He Himself was absolutely pure and undefiled, and as we keep company with Him we shall grow like Him. This is one of the great reasons why the Holy Spirit has come to indwell our hearts. He has come to make us like Christ. We're changed into His likeness, Paul says, from one degree of glory to another, for this comes from the Lord who is the Spirit.

And as it takes place, God becomes more real to us, and His fellowship more precious. "Strive for ... holiness" says Hebrews chapter 12, "without which no one will see the Lord" (v.14). That's seeing Him now. We don't have to wait until we get to heaven. Oh no, if we purify ourselves as He is pure, God will become very real to us now. We will live our lives in the light of His presence, and there is no joy to compare with that.

If you turn to the first chapter of John's first epistle you will find that's the very thing he is emphasizing. "Our fellowship is with the Father and with His Son Jesus Christ. And we are writing this that your joy may be complete" (RSV Margin). May the Lord lead us all into this completeness of joy. But let us remember it's only possible as we walk in the light. We must resolve we'll set our hearts on, and fill our minds with, whatever is true and honourable and just and pure and lovely and of good report, and then we shall prove His words true, "Blessed are the pure in heart, for they shall see God."

"Blessed are the peacemakers"

We come now to the seventh of the blessings that Jesus pronounced in His Sermon on the Mount: "Blessed are the peacemakers, for they shall be called sons of God."

We live in a world that is desperately seeking peace. But we hear more about war and unrest than we do about peace. Men have done their best to bring peace among the nations many of them honest and sincere men but still it eludes them. Tension grows and nations prepare for war. Why? Why are peace-loving men so unable to establish peace? Because the problem is not political or social, it is rooted deep in the human heart - the problem of sin, for men's hearts are full of lust and greed and selfishness. "There is no peace, says my God, for the wicked." God said that hundreds of years ago through His prophet Isaiah (Isaiah 57:21), and He said it twice over so that men would pay particular attention. And it is as true today as when Isaiah first spoke it. There can be no peace where there is sin.

But God is the great Peacemaker. He is the God of peace. That is one of His lovely titles. And to make peace He sent His Son. "Glory to God in the highest, and on earth peace among men" the angels said as they proclaimed His birth. But His birth alone could not bring peace, nor even His perfect life. Sin had to be dealt with before peace could come. So the Prince of peace went on His lonely way to Calvary, and there He made peace through the blood of His cross. "He was wounded for our transgressions, He was bruised for our iniquities: the chastisement of our peace was upon Him" (Isaiah 53:5 RV). Oh, how we love Him! He made peace. And then He preached peace, to those who were far off, to the many of us who are Gentiles, and to those who were near, our Jewish friends, and through Him we both have our access in one Spirit to the Father.

And now He calls us to the same great work in which He and His Father have been engaged. "Blessed are the peacemakers, for they shall be called sons of God." What a contemplation! You and I can become like God, for that is what it means to be called sons of God as we're engaged in the same glorious work of bringing peace into other people's lives. Being justified by faith we have peace with God ourselves, and now we long that others should find the same peace, first with God and then with their fellows.

Christian, are you a peacemaker? Are you introducing others to the Saviour who died to make their peace with God? And then among your Christian friends are you looking for opportunities of making peace?

"Blessed are those who are persecuted"

We have noticed that Jesus' blessing is promised not on anything we do, but on what we are. It is Christian character that is highlighted in the beatitudes. And we have seen also that the things He values are just the opposite of what the world values. For instance, what time have men in the world got for those who are poor in spirit? "Believe in yourself; push yourself forward;" that's what people say today. But Jesus teaches us differently. When the Holy Spirit works in our hearts and produces these characteristics, He makes us like Christ. And that immediately makes us different from other people who don't know Him.

The Christian is different. We have to recognize that. And because we are different we may well meet with ridicule and opposition. I'm sure that's why Jesus added an eighth blessing, for He went on to say, "Blessed are those who are persecuted for righteousness' sake, for theirs is the kingdom of heaven." Notice, it is those who are persecuted for righteousness' sake. We might be persecuted for other reasons; because of our unwise behaviour, for instance, or even because we hold strong views on certain points. But Jesus said, "Blessed are you when men revile you and persecute you and utter all kinds of evil against you falsely on my account" or "for My sake." It is when we suffer for His sake he promises the blessing.

Many of our Christian brothers and sisters are suffering for His sake today. Many live in lands where they are denied the freedom to worship and serve the Lord as the Bible teaches. And they are suffering simply because they love the Lord Jesus and they are not afraid to say so. We remember Jesus said, "If the world hates you, know that it has hated Me before it hated you. If you were of the world, the world would love its own; but because you are not of the world, but I chose you out of the world, therefore the world hates you … If they persecuted Me, they will persecute you" (John 15:18-20).

And we shall find that is true, in measure at any rate, in whatever land we live. "Indeed all who desire to live a godly life in Christ Jesus will be persecuted" wrote the apostle Paul to Timothy (2 Timothy 3:12). So take courage, Christian!

SUGGESTED PRAYER FOCUS

- For the strength to put away all impurity in our lives.
- For the peace of God that passes understanding to guard our hearts and minds.
- To be a peacemaker, even if that makes us a target by others.
- For readiness to be persecuted for Christ's sake and for the ability to rejoice when it happens.
- For those who are being persecuted for Jesus around the world today.

STUDY QUESTIONS

1. Read Titus 2 :14 and James 4:8. If God has already purified us, why do we need to purify ourselves?

2. Read 1 John 3:2-3. Why should this future hope cause us to purify ourselves now?

3. Read Titus 1:14-16. In what sense is nothing pure to the unbeliever? Can you think of any modern-day examples?

4. What forms might persecution of Christians take in the Western world versus other parts of the world? Is this changing ?

5. If we're not persecuted as Christians, individually or collectively, does that indicate something about us? See 2 Timothy 3:12.

6. Should we actively put ourselves in the path of persecution or seek to avoid it where possible? E.g. in relation to standing up for God's moral standards in society.

7. Could there possibly be a positive side to being persecuted? See James 1:3, Acts 5:41, 2 Corinthians 12:10.

8. What things are proper for a Christian be persecuted for and what are improper? See 1 Peter 4:12-16.

9. Read Hebrews 12:14a. Are there times where we have to choose between being at peace with God and at peace with men?

10. Should we ever compromise in order to achieve peace?

11. Read Matthew 10:34-36. Isn't this a strange thing for the Prince of Peace to say?

12. Read Romans 8:6. Why is the opposite of death 'life AND peace' here?

<u>STUDY NOTES</u>

5: LET YOUR LIGHT SHINE
(MATTHEW 5:13-16)

A group of young people were discussing the text, "You are the salt of the earth" and one suggestion after another was made as to the meaning of salt in this verse. "Salt preserves from decay," said one of them. "Salt imparts a desirable flavour," suggested another. Then a Chinese girl spoke out of her experience. "Salt creates thirst" she said, and there was sudden hush in the room. Everyone was thinking, "Have I ever made anyone thirsty for Jesus Christ?"

That is the text I want to consider with you now. We have been thinking about the beatitudes and noticing the blessing that Jesus promised to those who display this Christian character which the Holy Spirit produces in us. It is not something we can do ourselves, for it is the fruit of the Holy Spirit's work in our hearts. And we have noticed also that it's bound to make us different from those who have never accepted Christ as their Saviour.

In His teaching which followed, Jesus emphasized this difference. We are as different as salt is from the food it preserves. As different as light is from the darkness it dispels. But He doesn't take us out of the world because we are different. Not immediately anyway. One day He will. But meantime He leaves us here to be an influence for good. I believe that is the first thing we learn from our text, "You are the salt of the earth."

The implication is that the world is corrupt, corrupted as a result of sin. The whole world lies in the evil one, the Bible says. Sin has done its corrupting work in the lives of men and women. We see its effects all around us. But God expects us to be an influence for good, and to help prevent the spread of corruption; to have the effect salt has, of preserving the world from going thoroughly bad. If we are living the sort of life the beatitudes speak of, then that's the effect our lives will have. A very small quantity of salt is required to preserve a large amount of meat. And it's amazing how widely the influence of one Christian can be felt, if he or she is really living for Christ. You may be the only Christian in your workshop or office, but if you are not afraid to witness for Christ, the influence of your life will be felt by all. Have you ever noticed how the conversation can change when a Christian walks into a room? I have. His presence acts like salt.

And that was a good point another of the young people made that salt gives food a desirable flavour. Without it some foods can be quite insipid. Yes, if we are living the new life others will be attracted to it. "You've got something I haven't got," said a young lady to a friend of mine who worked in the same office. She had been watching his life and realized he'd got what she'd been wanting for so long. What a good thing it was, for her sake, that the salt had not lost its savour, or in other words, that my friend was really enjoying Christ and living the new life in front of his colleagues.

Which brings us to the excellent point the Chinese girl made that salt creates thirst. And we ask ourselves the searching question, "How many have become thirsty for Jesus because they've seen the difference He's made in my life?" May His word come with force to each of our hearts today. "You are the salt of the earth; but if the salt has lost its taste, how shall its saltiness be restored?" Let us pray for one another today, that our love for Christ may grow and that God will use us to influence other lives for Him.

"You are the light of the world"

When I was in Burma, on national holidays a group of us used to go to surrounding towns and villages carrying the gospel message. We would fill the gospel van and sing hymns as we travelled. "There's a call comes ringing o'er the restless wave, send the light, send the light. There are souls to rescue, there are souls to save, send the light, send the light" was one of our favourites. We were four nationalities, Burmese, Chinese, Indian and British, so there weren't many people we could not speak to along the way. Great days they were, bringing the light of the gospel to those who lived in darkness and superstition.

It reminds me of what Jesus said, "You are the light of the world. A city set on a hill cannot be hid. Nor do men light a lamp and put it under a bushel, but on a stand, and it gives light to all in the house. Let your light so shine before men, that they may see your good works and give glory to your Father who is in heaven." He was speaking to His disciples, but His words are true of all who follow Him. "Once you were darkness," wrote the apostle Paul to the Ephesians, "but now you are light in the Lord" (Ephesians 5:8).

Have you received light from Christ? He is the light who lights every man, coming into the world. Has He lit your lamp? Some people profess to show others the way, but they have never made personal contact with Christ themselves. "I am the light of the world," Jesus said (John 8:12). He is the only light in this dark world. There's no light apart from Him, and if we are going to light others along the way, we must first of all receive light from Christ.

The world is a dark place, despite the enlightenment men claim. It's true that the last century has brought a vast increase in knowledge, and knowledge brings light, they say. In many ways it does. Increased knowledge throws greater light on many subjects. But that is intellectual. It doesn't bring light in the heart. The spiritual darkness is as deep as ever. Jesus said, "He who follows Me will not walk in darkness, but will have the light of life." That is the light we need, light along life's way, light about the future, so that when we come to die we know where we're going. Friend, have you got the light? Then let it shine to others, so that in the dark places of the earth men and women may see the beauty of the Saviour and be helped to put their trust in Him.

The call of human hearts is ringing out today, urgently, desperately. Can you not hear it, Christian? Of course you can. Then send the light; send the light. "Let your light so shine before men." Jesus was speaking to a group of men who were later described as unlearned and ignorant. I don't think it was said disparagingly. They simply had not the benefit of advanced education, as had some of their contemporaries. But the men who said it noticed they'd been with Jesus, and that very fact had made a tremendous difference to their lives. They had come into contact with the One who is the Light of the World, and He had lit their lamps and now they were shining with the light which Christ gives.

God is light, the Bible says. That is what He is essentially. His whole Being is light. In Him is no darkness at all. And Jesus is God, equal in every way with His Father. He also is light. When He came into the world He said, "I am the light of the world." He came to shine in its darkness and to show us the way to heaven. The world is a dark place, morally and spiritually dark. It's dark with sin. When Jesus came as the light of the world, He showed up sin for what it was. And the result? He was unwanted hated because of it and eventually men crucified Him outside their capital city. "This is the judgement," Jesus said, "that the light has come into the world, and men loved darkness rather than light, because their deeds were evil" (John 3:19). But there were some who believed on Him, who were willing to be turned from darkness to light. They followed Christ and He have them the light of life. And to them He said, "You are the light of the world ... even so let your light shine before men."

Jesus used two figures, you'll notice. He spoke about a city set on a hill which cannot be hidden. And He spoke about a lamp on a stand shining to all in the house. One was seen a long distance away, and the other close up. There is a sense in which each of us answers to both. A small light shining can be seen a long way off when it's dark, like a city on a hill. But someone has said, "The light that shines the farthest shines the brightest nearest home." If we are shining as God intends we should there will be a bright light shining amongst those to whom we are nearest, the folks we live with, the people we work amongst. But what does it really mean to let our light shine? In practical terms, how do we do it? The apostle Paul spelt it out to the Ephesians when he wrote, "The fruit of light is found in all that is good and right and true" (Ephesians 5:9). That's helpful, isn't it? Where these things are seen in our lives, the light shines out for all to see.

A missionary in India was teaching a group of children about Jesus and explaining how good and kind He is, how forgiving and merciful. She noticed a deepening interest on the children's part. And as she went on one little girl became extremely excited and jumping up she said, "I know him, I know him. He lives right near us." Wasn't that lovely! Whoever it was lived near them had been letting his light shine, and even the young children understood that. Even so let your light shine, that men may see your good works and glorify your Father who is in heaven.

SUGGESTED PRAYER FOCUS

- For our individual and collective saltiness in the world to be maintained.
- For those that have lost their saltiness, that God may graciously allow it to be restored.
- For the bravery to let our light shine in an increasingly dark world.
- For those that walk in the darkness, that God may use us to bring them into the light.

STUDY QUESTIONS

1. How can Christians lose their 'saltiness' in the world?
2. Is it really true that once that our 'saltiness' is lost, it can never be recovered?
3. How do we ensure our words are seasoned with salt (Colossians 4:6), without appearing overly sanctimonious or pious?
4. Jesus says in Mark 9:50, "Have salt in yourselves, and have peace with one another." Why did he link these two things?
5. Read Ezekiel 16:4. Rubbing a newborn with salt indicated that the child would be raised to have integrity and to always be truthful. How can our contact with people have the same positive effect?
6. Why is light not simply the opposite of darkness? (John 1:5)
7. Read Luke 11:35. How is it possible that the light that is within us is darkness?
8. Read 2 Corinthians 4:6 – from where does our light originate?
9. Read Ephesians 5:8-13. Consider the possibility that being the light of the world may bring unpopularity by exposing wickedness.

<u>STUDY NOTES</u>

6: IN DANGER OF HELLFIRE
(MATTHEW 5:21-37)

It has been said that "the Lord Jesus is God spelling Himself out in a language that man can understand." The Sermon on the Mount is a clear example of that principle. His message leaves no doubt as to the cost of discipleship. It is a faulty gospel that preaches remission without submission, alliance without allegiance. Christ does not reign where He does not rule. His teaching is as valid today as it will be in His future kingdom.

Murder and Anger Condemned

"But I say unto you, that every one who is angry with his brother shall be in danger of the judgement; and whosoever shall say to his brother, Raca, shall be in danger of the council; and whosoever shall say, you fool, shall be in danger of the hell of fire" (Matthew 5:22).

The Lord saw anger and name-calling to be of such a serious nature as to warrant severe judgement. Cain's anger was not placated until he had murdered his brother. Anger often runs close to the thin edge of violence; anger has frightening potential. Destructive anger and bad temper should have no place in the life of a disciple of Jesus. In addition to being a sin for which forgiveness must be sought, it has been known medically to be self-damaging physically. But Ephesians 4:26 does say, "be angry and do not sin." An expanded translation is, "angry with a righteous indignation", a healthy emotion when directed against sin and unrighteousness.

Removing the Barrier

"Therefore if you bring your gift to the altar, and there remember that your brother has something against you, leave your gift there before the altar, and go your way. First be reconciled to your brother, and then come and offer your gift" (Matthew 5:23-24).

A brother treated with contempt or ridicule is a brother injured. A conscious barrier is erected. However impeccable and sincere our worship and prayers, God will not accept them. So long as someone is the victim of mental cruelty by our slander or gossip, so long have we forfeited our communion with God. The wrong must be made right, and the love of Jesus allowed to flow again in healing and caring for that brother for whom Christ died. We need to remember that Jesus patiently bore the hatred, cruelty, slander and insults of men, and the fearful judgement of God for those very sins, that He might bring us into eternal fellowship and reconciliation with Himself and each other. For a man to say he loves God and in his heart hate his brother, is hypocritical.

"He that hates his brother is in the darkness ... If a man say, I love God, and hates his brother, he is a liar" (1 John 2:11; 4:20). In our experience, the equivalent of the "gift at the altar" is the Lord's table and the breaking of the bread on a Sunday morning. Reconciliation with an offended brother (or sister) must be made before sitting together in worship. Not only so, but whatever has caused the breach in relationships must also be dealt with by the offender. "Knowing this, that our old man was crucified with Him (Jesus)" (Romans 6:6) is a truth which makes its claim on our lives to expose anger, resentment, jealousy, pride, bitterness or any flesh-borne carnal sin, and bring it to the cross to be crucified.

Debtors

"Agree with your adversary quickly, while you are on the way with him, lest your adversary deliver you to the judge, the judge hand you over to the officer, and you be thrown into prison. Assuredly, I say to you, you will by no means get out of there till you have paid the last penny" (Matthew 5:25, 26).

This is a word picture of an ancient lawsuit, where the accuser and the accused were given the opportunity to walk together to the court, and on the way do everything possible to settle out of court. Reference by Jesus to this cultural practice urges a prompt settlement of debts, thus precluding legal action. It presupposes initially that there was a long-standing debt which necessitated court action. The word "adversary" used here, means "opponent, as in a court of law, or law suit."

Whether through poor business or domestic management or even circumstances beyond the control of the accused, the case was viewed by Jesus as serious. Litigation is not Jesus' alternative for a disciple in such a case. He laid down a principle for His people, that "out of court" settlement is established for such social irregularities as default in debts. Moreover, the debtor, once cleared of an obligation, must change his life style to avoid a repetition of long standing unpaid debts, which can only bring Christian testimony into disrepute. Romans 13:8 covers for all time the disciple's attitude towards debt: "Owe no man anything, save to love ..."

In our "buy now, pay later" society, some Christians may be amongst the millions who purchase on credit beyond their financial ability to pay, and are always in debt. This is clearly not in Jesus' will for His people.

Lust

"But I say to you that whoever looks at a woman to lust for her has already committed adultery with her in his heart." (Matthew 5:28). Jesus also said, "For out of the heart proceed evil thoughts, murders, adulteries, fornication ... These are the things which defile the man" (Matthew 15:19, 20). These hard-hitting words of Jesus touch all of us. His claims in discipleship demand absolute and uncompromising moral purity. Immoral actions are the result of immoral thinking. Whether committed in the secret closet of our mind, or physically, an immoral act is the tangible fruit of desire which forfeits our discipleship and a true following of Christ.

Accompanying destructive guilt feelings rob a Christian of his or her communion with God. Jesus' penetrating words reveal that an imagined sexual experience, flashed on our mental screen in secret, is of the same essential nature as the overt act. Continued unclean thoughts become habit forming, and sooner or later result in immoral action. Hebrews 13:4 warns that "fornicators and adulterers God will judge." King David's family and the whole kingdom of Israel were troubled for years after his affair with Bathsheba and the heartless murder of her innocent husband. "God is not mocked; for whatever a man sows, that he will also reap" (Galatians 6:7).

The joy and fulfilment of intimacy was designed by an all-wise Creator for marriage only. God's order for unblemished purity can only be safeguarded by walking daily with Jesus, reckoning ourselves "dead unto sin, but alive unto God in Christ Jesus" (Romans 6:11). Then, if someone does slip and fall into sin, is our attitude one of sorrow or harsh condemnation? Following scriptural action by the church, shouldn't there be prayer for a work of true repentance and restoration? When godly sorrow works repentance (2 Corinthians 7:10), "confirm your love toward him", writes Paul (2 Corinthians 2:8). If I mentally exalt myself above an erring brother or sister, by cultivating a secret satisfaction that it was someone else who fell, and not I, and lack the healing ministry of compassion, remembering my own weakness, then I know little of Christ's love at Calvary. If we abide in Him, we shall see everything through the eyes of Jesus in purity and holiness.

Cutting off the offending hand or plucking out the lustful eye has a teaching deeper than the physical. The hand or eye can't commit sins of themselves. The sinful motions of our members are slaves to the mind of the flesh. It is evil desire that motivates. Cutting off a hand would not remove the old nature of sin. This will of course always be with us in our earthly experience (Ephesians 4:22), although God sees it as having been crucified with Christ (Romans 6:6). We on our part must recognize the daily need to reckon ourselves dead unto sin, but alive unto God in Christ Jesus (Romans 6:14). For "those who are Christ's have crucified the flesh with its passions and desires" (Galatians 5:24).

Divorce

"But I say to you that whoever divorces his wife for any reason except sexual immorality causes her to commit adultery; and whoever marries a woman who is divorced commits adultery." (Matthew 5:32, also Matthew 19:9).

Matthew, the gospel to the Jew, is the only one that records the "excepting clause" in Jesus' statement on divorce. It is submitted that the fornication referred to by our Lord was in fact the sexual impurity Moses alluded to in Deuteronomy 22:14. This would have taken place with another man during the betrothal period, prior to the actual marriage ceremony. In Hebrew custom, betrothal meant that the woman was regarded as the man's wife. When Joseph discovered Mary was pregnant, he was minded to put her away. The angel's reassuring words put his troubled mind at rest. "Do not be afraid to take to you Mary your wife." Joseph no doubt had the Deuteronomy law in mind.

Jesus recognized Moses' law and it is clear that the "except for fornication" clause has reference to a couple in Israel who had not actually taken their marriage vows. Such understanding of the "exception" leaves us with Jesus' teaching, fully consistent with His divorce statements in both Mark and Luke, the universal law of God excludes divorce and re-marriage for any cause. "What God has joined together, let not man separate." This is a hard saying for the harsh reality of today's world. For the true believer it is the cost of discipleship, and let us remember that the word of God has all the right repair materials for troubled marriages. God's order for marriage and the family is designed to prevent divorce. Whatever the strains and unfulfilled expectations in Christian marriage, divorce is never an option in God's plan. Only the healing ministry of Christ's love can provide the spiritual and emotional flame that will whenever necessary rekindle the love and joy of the permanent commitment to Jesus and each other in the sacred covenant of marriage.

Truth

"Again you have heard that it was said to those of old, 'You shall not swear falsely, but shall perform your oaths to the Lord.' But I say to you, do not swear at all: neither by heaven, for it is God's throne; nor by the earth, for it is His footstool; nor by Jerusalem, for it is the city of the great King. Nor shall you swear by your head, because you cannot make one hair white or black. But let your 'Yes' be 'Yes,' and your 'No,' 'No.' For whatever is more than these is from the evil one." (Matthew 5:33-37).

Perjury was forbidden in Israel, under the law (Leviticus 19:12). The oath was given because of man's fallen sinful nature. It showed something was wrong. It admitted the possibility of lies. Jesus showed in the new law of the kingdom of heaven that pure truth needs no oath. Truth, as in Jesus, sets it above all possibility of falsehood. Only in the new nature in Christ is complete truth possible. Only as His disciples are totally committed to Him and He dwells within (John 14:23), can truth remain constant in our hearts. He has taught us that we should say and mean "Yes" or "No" and never equivocate. Every Christian's moral and business ethics must have a basis of uncompromising honesty and truthfulness.

SUGGESTED PRAYER FOCUS

- For help to guard against loose and harmful speech.
- To be able to earn a reputation for honesty and truthfulness in all the spheres of life.
- For strong, loving Christian marriages to be protected and grace to be given to those who are in struggling relationships.
- To be good stewards of our resources and be self-sufficient.

STUDY QUESTIONS

1. If Jesus did not come to abolish the law (Matthew 5:17), why are believers no longer under the law (Romans 6:14)?
2. Read Matthew 5:19. Did Jesus mean that some commandments are more important than others, or something else? (Hint: it's something else!)
3. What is the essential difference between righteous anger and sinful anger? Support your answer using examples of the righteous anger of God and Jesus.
4. The world offers anger management courses – how can the Christian 'manage' his/her anger biblically?
5. Read Matthew 5:22. Does calling someone a fool really endanger your soul?
6. Why doesn't committing adultery in the heart carry the same church discipline as committing the actual physical act?
7. In what practical ways can we avoid adultery of the heart? (See Job 31:1)
8. Read Matthew 5:29-30: Are there any cases where these verses could/should be taken literally and not simply figuratively (e.g. medical castration)?
9. Should a Christian feel able to take an oath in a court of law?
10. How do you explain God's use of an oath in Hebrews 6:17?

STUDY NOTES

7: TURN THE OTHER CHEEK
(MATTHEW 5:38-48)

In this passage, Jesus continues His instructions to those who would be his disciples and compares that which they'd been given in the past with the newer and higher standards that He was now laying on them. The Matthew passage is closely paralleled by that in Luke 6:27-35, but with significant differences. The Law had been given to a people to guide them to God's standards. Paul says that the Law had been a tutor to bring us to Christ (Galatians 3:24) and if it had been followed it would have infallibly led God's people to His Son. Sadly, the Law had been added to by well-meaning but misled teachers who, by so doing, had diverted people from the Christ whom He'd sent. Conditions laid down by God which were within the grasp of a holy people had been so restricted and added to that they put them outside their grasp. Jesus, however, was now giving His disciples new guidelines capable of being followed only by a people who had the Spirit of the new life within them, a gift which God alone could give. In future, they were to "repay no one evil for evil" (Romans 12:17).

An Eye for an Eye

"An eye for an eye and a tooth for a tooth" (v.48) had certainly been God's instruction in a past day. Modern thinkers will be inclined to treat this as a barbaric statement, but nothing could be further from the truth. It was God's limitation upon the retribution that would otherwise be exacted. The natural man would have gone much further and have taken a life for an eye when he exacted vengeance. Witness the boasting words of Lamech as early as Genesis 4:23-24. He would kill a man who wounded him or even only bruised him and he would be avenged seventy times for any slight that he was offered! God's law in Exodus 21:24 was itself a limit which some men might naturally wish to overstep. Jesus goes even further in restricting vengeance.

"Whoever slaps you on your right cheek, turn the other to him also." It is noteworthy that, in Luke, Jesus does not specify which cheek is struck first. In the case of a right-handed man facing his opponent, a blow on the right cheek could only be delivered with the back of the hand and as such would not be particularly hard, it would be more in the nature of an insult. Jesus says, "Turn the other cheek." The blow would then be immeasurably harder. It is possible that the phraseology used by Jesus in Matthew indicates a legal form of assault (as for instance in verse 40), but the Luke scripture shows that no matter which cheek is struck first, and therefore no matter how hard the blow, there is to be no retaliation, but rather "pray for those that spitefully use you" (Luke 6:28).

Debtors and creditors

In verse 40, Jesus specifically refers to a man going to law against a disciple. He reminds them that the Law would permit a creditor to take a man's coat (inner garment – "chiton" in the Greek), but did not permit him to take a man's cloak (outer garment – "himation" in the Greek) with the intention of depriving him of it permanently. In both Exodus 22:26-27 and Deuteronomy 24:10-13 there is a specific limitation to damages that may be recovered in that a man's outer garment must be returned to him at nightfall so that he could use it as a covering. Even if the debt is not fully paid by the sale of all the other pledges, the debtor must be left with something to keep him warm at night.

This limitation has been accepted down the ages and even today in enlightened countries a debtor must be left with something to protect him. But Jesus tells His disciples here not to stand on their legal rights. If you are indebted and cannot pay, accept all your goods being taken, no matter what personal discomfort you will have to endure. The Luke scripture does not deal with the legal side. In this case force is being used, so that the outer garment is taken first. Even in such cases Jesus says "no retaliation." You are to give your assailant the inner garment as well. You do not ask if he really needs it or whether he is using violence for its own sake. Jesus Himself was to lose both such garments at the cross (John 19:23-24). The Psalmist had foretold this in Psalm 22:18 and Jesus would not allow one word of

Scripture to fall to the ground unfulfilled.

The Extra Mile

To be compelled to go one mile (verse 41) was the limit that the Roman authorities could place upon anyone. It was legally enforceable and the impressing into service of Simon of Cyrene is a case in point. Jesus again says: do not stand upon your legal rights - go even further if the Roman or other authorities require you to. To be compelled to do anything that the hated occupiers of the land demanded was an affront to all Jews. No wonder the multitudes who overheard what Jesus was saying were astonished at His teaching (Matthew 7:28).

The instructions in verse 42 were to be even more difficult for His disciples. The application of verses 38 to 41 might be theoretical only. One might never be attacked or in debt or compelled to do anything against one's will, but "the poor you have with you always" (John 12:8) and would-be borrowers there will always be in plenty. The Psalmist had spoken of those who borrow and never repay and of the righteous who gave and lent graciously. "His seed is blessed", said David (Psalm 37:21, 26). The natural man would say that both he and his seed would suffer if this precept were to be followed, but "I have been young, and now am old; yet I have not seen the righteous forsaken, nor his descendants begging bread." (Psalm 37:25).

It's noteworthy here that in Luke Jesus adds the words "and just as you want men to do to you, you also do to them likewise." (Luke 6:31), words found in Matthew 7:12, where Jesus confirms that "this is the law and the prophets." What we are to do is positive, not negative. The natural man would say "Don't do to others what you wouldn't want done to yourself." Jesus urges us to think first of all the things that we would like to have done to us and then go out and do them to others. This is honoured more in the breach than the observance, but Jesus reminds His disciples of their heavenly Father whose giving is without stint even to those who never repay. This giving was to be expressed in its fullest measure when "He gave His only begotten Son."

Love Your Neighbour

In verse 43, Jesus reminds them, "You shall love your neighbour." This they had known from of old. Leviticus 19:18 and the last five commandments all pointed to this end. One young man could say, "All these things have I observed," (Matthew 19:20) and there can be no doubt that many had done their utmost to live by this precept. However, the Jewish teachers had added "hate your enemy." This was an unwarrantable addition to Scripture. No doubt those responsible had thought it was a justifiable extension to Deuteronomy 23:6, but any addition to Scripture will bring its own punishment. Eve's failure in this respect by adding "nor shall you touch it" (Genesis 3:3) had helped to bring about her own downfall.

Once we add to God's word we effectively say, "Our word is as good as God's" and once that door is opened there is no end to the heresies that are introduced. Jesus removes the addition completely. They were to pray for their enemies and persecutors just as Jesus did on the cross and as Stephen did when he, too, was persecuted for righteousness' sake.

If one follows all these precepts, says Jesus, "You therefore shall be perfect (complete), even as your heavenly Father is perfect." He makes His blessings to fall upon the just and the unjust alike. If He were to limit His rain and sunshine to the righteous only, there would be little enough upon the tables of those who did not know Him. God had suffered such insolence and disrespect from man whom He had made, and was to suffer even more deeply when His Son was so shamefully treated on the cross. Yet He still provided for those who hated Him and so also should those who profess to be disciples of Christ.

Note verse 45: "that you may be sons of your Father in heaven." Paul sets out the difference between "children" and "sons" in Romans 8:14-21: "For as many as are led by the Spirit of God, these are sons of God. For you did not receive the spirit of bondage again to fear, but you received the Spirit of adoption by whom we cry out, "Abba, Father." The Spirit Himself bears witness with our spirit that we are children of God, and if children, then heirs - heirs of God and joint heirs with Christ, if indeed we suffer with Him, that we may also be glorified together."

All believers have been baptized in one Spirit and are children of God. On the other hand "as many as are led by the Spirit of God, these are sons of God." Their conduct is the evidence of their relationship and their likeness to His character. These words emphasize yet once again that the "Sermon on the Mount" was addressed to disciples of Jesus and not to the multitudes who stood around.

SUGGESTED PRAYER FOCUS

- For grace to treat our "enemies" as well as our friends.
- For help to strive for God's perfection, not man's mediocrity.
- For the presence of mind not to retaliate when provoked or attacked, but turn the other cheek.

STUDY QUESTIONS

1. Read Matthew 5:39. How far do we take the principle of non-resistance? What would you do, for example, if someone threatened to kidnap your family?
2. Does this passage rule out a Christian engaging in war, even what might be considered to be a just war?
3. Do you have any personal experience of putting Matthew 5:39-42 into practice? What was the outcome?
4. How does Jesus' example laid out in 1 Peter 2:23 help us?
5. Is it appropriate for Christians to view anyone as their enemy?
6. Read Proverbs 25:22. What should our motives and objectives be in dealing with our "enemies" – shaming, revenge or something else?
7. In Matthew 5:48, Jesus instructs us to be perfect as the Father is perfect. Is this realistic? What does he mean?

<u>STUDY NOTES</u>

8: SEEK GOD'S APPROVAL, NOT MAN'S!
(MATTHEW 6:1-18)

I n this part of the Sermon on the Mount, Jesus concentrates our thoughts on three areas of our individual lives in which our actions may be wrongly or rightly motivated according to whether we seek the approval of men or the glory of God:

Giving to the needy - ALMS
Speaking to God - PRAYER
Disciplining ourselves - FASTING

In each area He tells us firstly what not to do and then what we should do. This is surely sound psychology, to put last what He wants to leave with us, to emphasize. Further, the relative amount of space allotted to each area is telling: one fifth to each of alms and fasting and three fifths to prayer. In other words, three times as much weight is placed on our dealings with God as with our dealings with our fellow men or ourselves. This chapter follows the same pattern in both respects.

Giving to the Needy

There were those in Jerusalem at the time of Jesus who organized a fanfare as a prelude to their almsgiving, to impress their neighbours and friends. In today's world there are still those who will "blow their own trumpet," in respect of giving to charity, and some will ensure that their names appear on a subscription list. Jesus said that people would never receive the Father's recognition of their gift, if in the making of it they are seeking the glory of men. In this context, the collection box in the meeting place of the church is best placed so that giving can be secret, in case an element of temptation should arise in this sense.

In making His positive appeal on giving, Jesus used a saying which has become very common "Let not your left hand know what your right hand is doing." Jesus meant it to apply to individuals and individual giving. When we apply it to ourselves, may it find us cheerfully liberal and not calculating, so that the Father can approve our gift (2 Corinthians 9:7).

Speaking to God

There were those in Jerusalem at the time of Jesus who prayed publicly in the street to obtain the approval of passers-by. In today's Western world this rarely happens. In Muslim countries, public kneeling and bowing towards Mecca is common and is likely to be sincere. It does, however, provide temptation for the hypocrite and seems to be far removed from the Lord's answer to the question, "Where shall I pray?" To obtain the Father's approval, prayer must be private, behind closed doors, where He alone can see and where for us, there are fewer distractions.

Moving on to "How shall I pray?", Jesus indicates it should certainly not be at great length if we are thinking that God will be appeased by many words. Such volubility, for the insincere, could be an opportunity for display before men and for self-centredness as opposed to God-centredness. In the wonderful example of prayer which the Lord then gave, two features stand out clearly: not only is it short - just seven themes - but it is more God centred than man-centred as the following summary reveals:

GOD
1. Our Father in heaven
2. Hallowed be Thy name
3. Thy kingdom come: Thy will be done on earth as it is in heaven

MAN
4. Give us today our daily bread
5. Forgive us our debts as we forgive our debtors
6. Lead us not into temptation but deliver us from evil

GOD
7. For Thine is the kingdom the power and the glory for ever, Amen.

God first and God last. He is the Alpha and the Omega. Even the requests relative to man involve God's action.

- Who but God provides food for mankind?
- Who can forgive debts or sins but God? (The Lord expands on this subject in verses 14 and 15, where it is made clear that His forgiveness of our sins is dependent on our forgiveness of our fellows' sins.)
- Who can be delivered from the evil one without the power that comes from God?

So God-centredness should characterize our prayer life. When we really put God at the forefront of our thoughts immediately our own shortcomings are apparent and we are moved to confession, which is a fitting prelude to all our speaking to God. As we continue to keep God in the vanguard of our meditations all His goodness passes before us and thanksgiving and praise ensue. As we review His vast resources our requests pour out, and Scripture is full of examples of the wide range of the same. Hezekiah (2 Kings 19:14) spread before the Lord a national problem; Hannah (1 Samuel 1) a very personal problem; the apostle Paul (Ephesians 1:16) didn't cease to make mention of the saints in prayer.

Similar examples could be multiplied. Some have expressed difficulty in reconciling the fact that Jesus spent whole nights in prayer, with the shortness of the sample prayer of Matthew 6. However, as seen above, when the God-first pattern of that prayer is applied it evokes such extensive exercise that we may wonder if a night is long enough! Then many words are very much acceptable to the Father.

We may now ask what is the place in all this for the use of the actual words which are contained in the sample prayer which Jesus gave us? Since it is essentially a "God and me" prayer and the Scripture encourages us to "each count others better than ourselves," perhaps we should therefore put our prayers for ourselves last. This may be suggesting to us that we should on occasion repeat the sample prayer at the end of our sessions of speaking to God.

Disciplining Ourselves

The hypocrites of Jesus' times used fasting as a means of attracting attention to themselves. The real benefit from such denial, however, can only be gauged by the extent to which it brings glory to God. Jesus insists that it should be done unobtrusively, attracting the attention of the Father only. Quite often fasting is linked with prayer (Daniel 9:3; Matthew 17:21 RVM; Mark 9:29 RVM; Luke 2:37; Acts 14:23) if the one is to be done in secret, so should the other. Restraint in the indulgence of fleshly appetites can sharpen appreciation of spiritual values and only if this is the end-product is the discipline worthwhile.

Epilogue

Jesus told a short parable recorded in Luke 18:9-14. A Pharisee and a publican went into the Temple to pray. The Pharisee's prayer could not be more boastfully self-centred:

> I thank You that I am not like other men - PRAYER
> I fast twice a week - FASTING
> I give tithes of all I possess - ALMS

The same three areas of individual righteousness appear as

have been discussed from the Sermon on the Mount. As far as the Father was concerned, the Pharisee's prayer, fasting or alms made no impact. The publican humbly said, "God be merciful to me a sinner." He went to his house justified rather than the Pharisee.

SUGGESTED PRAYER FOCUS

- To be more aware of, and less content with, our own hypocrisy.
- To protect our motives for everything we do, and keep them pure.
- For our public persona to match our private life, and vice-versa.
- To be more forgiving and understanding of the faults and shortcomings of others.
- To be able to pray to God with complete honesty and sincerity.
- To avoid prayer degenerating into a "shopping list", rather than an opportunity to adore, commune, confess and thank.

STUDY QUESTIONS

1. In what areas today are we possibly at greatest risk of acting like the Pharisees?
2. We might not blow trumpets before doing good these days, but in what more subtle ways can we boast about our actions?
3. How do we reconcile doing good deeds in secret with letting our light shine before men?
4. In what way will God openly reward secret giving (Matthew 6:4), and how will it be known it is He who does so?
5. If God knows what we need before we pray (Matthew 6:8), then why bother asking?
6. What does it means to pray that God's kingdom will come (Matthew 6:10)?
7. Why ask God not to lead us into temptation (Matthew 6:13) – would he ever do something like that?
8. Why will God only forgive our sins if we forgive others (Matthew 6:14-15) – isn't forgiveness a matter between us and Him?
9. What is the purpose of fasting?
10. Is fasting something we should be doing as Christians today?

<u>STUDY NOTES</u>

9: YOUR HEART IS WHERE YOUR TREASURE IS
(MATTHEW 6:19-34)

Jesus' discourse from verse nineteen to the end of chapter 6 of Matthew has to do with worldliness and the relationship of the disciple to the world. If the follower of Jesus doesn't overcome the world, as his Lord did (John 16:33), the world will overcome him. The deceitfulness of worldly riches and the anxiety often resulting from the pursuit of material possessions choke the effect and power of God's word (Matthew 13:22).

Life's True Quest

Man's life at best is uncertain; there is no assurance he will live the years he would like to. Worldly-minded men calculate success in terms of wealth accumulation and physical comforts. Disciples of Jesus may themselves do the same. The rat-race for advancement, the struggle for yet more is unending like a sea which cannot be filled (Ecclesiastes 1:7).

Greed can never get enough, worry can never have enough. Of course, possessions can represent a danger to those without them, as much as to those who have them. The life of the disciple is spoiled when absorbed in the pursuit of material things; it is blessed when spiritual things are given priority. This principle is illustrated in Matthew's own life. In response to Christ's call, he turned his back upon a lucrative position in an earthly kingdom, and was rewarded by being appointed an apostle of Jesus and a chronicler of a spiritual kingdom. Like Matthew, God's kingdom must be the principal passion in the heart of the disciple. It is his privilege to witness to the world that he is of a different spirit from the "man of the world".

True Wealth

To set one's heart upon earthly treasures (Matthew 6:19) is to live in perpetual insecurity. They can be the target of thieves or damaged by the ravages of insects, and are always subject to natural forces of destruction. Men plan their lives to provide security for themselves. Careful management and business prudence are not censured by Jesus. What is open to His stricture is the misguided valuation of perishable earthly treasure compared with eternal heavenly treasure. "Laying up" conveys the thought of hoarding, storing goods. Though invisible and intangible, the "real" treasure is the reward awaiting those whose lives have been "rich toward God" (Luke 12:21) i.e. rich where God is concerned, and "rich in faith" (James 2:5); lives marked by patience, perseverance and holiness, having submitted to the perfect control of a heavenly Father.

Jesus is not calling for successful opportunists; such are applauded by fellow-aspirants in worldly affairs where doubtful dealings and shady transactions often characterize the unscrupulous activities of men "without Christ". Onus for responsible action is placed upon the individual disciple. Jesus isn't rebuking or warning against the ownership of wealth. He is emphasizing that the lives of His followers mustn't be dominated by the desire for wealth. Trust in riches and trust in God are incompatible. The "heart" and "treasure" go together. A person's heart is always with his treasure that which he most values. The path of true happiness is the path of Christlikeness. The futility of earthly treasure-seeking and what it may lead to are well illustrated in the story of Joshua 7 concerning Achan. Man has only one heart and the thing upon which it is set will reveal his true spirit.

A Correct Focus

The disciple's "outlook" is to be clear and unequivocal. The eye is the lamp of the body. The body is directed by what the eye sees. Using metaphorical language, Jesus speaks of the "single" eye and the "evil" eye (Matthew 6:22-23). The one is contrasted with the other. The single eye is the enlightened eye, seeing as God sees through the operation of His word in the heart (Ephesians 5:8). As the "lamp of the body", its beam is directed by the Holy Spirit so that light is shed on what is valuable and worthwhile to God. The evil or diseased eye presents to the mind and heart a false set of values.

Therefore, if the only light to enter through the vehicle of the eye is perverted then the darkness which is in our body through sin in our nature is total indeed. A wrong assessment clouds the vision of permanent spiritual realities. True treasure-seeking is not "seeing only what is near", what has to do with the present - man's day (2 Peter 1:9), but "looking for God's day". This "outlook" is achieved by diligence in Christian living.

Undivided Service

Having spoken of the tragedy of absorption with earthly riches and the necessity for true value-judgements, Jesus then referred to decisive and committed service to one Master. To attempt to serve two masters must fail and confusion is caused to the servant. Men cannot be servants of God and wealth at the same time. One of two possible attitudes may be adopted: (1) despising wealth for its own sake and loving God: (2) loving money and goods and despising God. They cannot co-exist. Single ownership and full-time service are the essentials of the work of a slave. God requires complete allegiance and undivided loyalty. Accumulating wealth eventually enslaves those whose time is absorbed with this pursuit. "Him only you shall serve" (Matthew 4:10).

The Futility of Anxiety

The last ten verses of Matthew 6 can be subdivided into three parts, each preceded by the words "Be not ... anxious". Pointedly, Jesus continues. Not only does covetousness lead men to hoard material possessions, but also causes undue anxiety as to the future for themselves and their dependants. The Authorised Version rendering, "Take no thought" isn't a condemnation of forward planning, but an exhortation to disciples of Jesus not to fret over the future. Worry dishonours God and betrays unbelief. It assumes we are better able to manage our affairs than God. It is putting self first. It indicates a detached existence from our Creator God and our Heavenly Father. Anxieties allowed and indulged may become habitual.

The absence of anxiety does not bring starvation to the creatures of the air. They are not idle or unwise. They work hard building nests, feeding their young, but do not fret or fuss. In Luke 12 the bird mentioned is the raven an unclean bird (Leviticus 11:15). They are without the faculty to sow, reap or garner into barns, yet they are cared for. "They wait upon God's bounty to receive their food in due season." They gather what God has given (Psalm 104:27-28). "He gives to the creature his food" (Psalm 147:9). The Lord's own are of much more value (Matthew 6:26). The flowers with which God beautifies the countryside display His lavishness in a beauty that Solomon's magnificent robes could never match. The God of the universe is not indifferent to any part of His creation. Even the grass of the field He clothes (v.30).

"Be not anxious therefore for your life ... your body." Both are God's property. What God does for inanimate nature and the lower creatures is sufficient incentive to keep His own from corroding care.

The Principal Pursuit

The incessant restlessness of those who give no recognition to God's superintending providence serves as a salutary object lesson (Matthew 6:32). The disciple has a heavenly Father - a meaningful designation describing all the power of Heaven at His command and all the loving sympathy of a Father who knows the essential needs of His own. Getting the priorities right is a life-time's work. The priority for the disciple is succinctly stated: "Seek ye first His kingdom." This is where concentrated action is to be centred, not precluding legitimate effort in "all these (other) things." But the heart mustn't be set on the latter. God may not necessarily give us what we want but He gives what is best.

The disciple must cultivate a determined attitude, inner resolution, singlemindedness, an undivided heart and a desire to work towards God's rule in the hearts of men (His kingdom) and the establishment of His justice and mercy in their lives (His righteousness). The words of Jeremiah the prophet to Baruch carry a timeless voice. "Do you seek great things for yourself? Seek them not" (Revised Standard Version). Rather, "Seek first ... God."

SUGGESTED PRAYER FOCUS

- That we will cast our burdens on the Lord (Psalm 55:22).
- That we will set our minds on things above, not on things on the earth (Colossians 3:2).
- That we will not be unstable, double-minded Christians (James 1:8).

STUDY QUESTIONS

1. Should we consciously be trying to lay up treasure in heaven, or is that a wrong motive for our actions?

2. How can you tell what your heart treasures the most?

3. Is it wrong to prepare for our earthly future by using pension plans and other investments?

4. Is it wrong to be rich? Where there any people in the Bible who were rich AND righteous?

5. What is Mammon (Matthew 6:24)?

6. Does Matthew 6:25-30 imply that one does not have to work for a living but instead rely on God to provide? (but see 2 Thessalonians 3:10)

7. Is there a practical difference between worry and concern (see 2 Corinthians 11:28)?

8. What could worrying greatly about something be a symptom of?

STUDY NOTES

10: LOVE YOUR NEIGHBOUR
(MATTHEW 7:1-12)

"Therefore, whatever you want men to do to you, do also to them, for this is the Law and the Prophets." (Matthew 7:12).

Love your neighbour
Our text, this key verse from the Sermon on the Mount, concisely expresses the practical form that Christlikeness should take in our actions towards others. Its context, the inappropriateness of earthly anxiety, demonstrates the additional effect that its practice will have upon ourselves. Jesus had just finished telling His listeners that He had come to fulfil the law and the prophets. This summation of both of these, closely resembling the royal law of

James 2:8, epitomizes His desire for the behaviour of all who would be sons (and daughters) of the Kingdom.

Leviticus 19:18 is quoted seven times in the New Testament, each time through its context revealing something further of the Person who fulfilled it, and giving further direction to those who would be His disciples: You shall love your neighbour as yourself. Matthew 5:44 adds the love of enemies; 19:21; responsibility to those less fortunate; 22:39, the impossibility of loving God without loving one's fellow. Mark 12:33 shows the superiority of love over sacrifices and offerings, while the quotation in Galatians 5:13-15 underscores its importance in our lives in fellowship with believers. Luke 10:25-37 stresses the necessity for action rather than passivity in its fulfilment, and James 2:8-9 shows how that fulfilment requires special care. Matthew 7 begins with the need for a correct estimation of the character of others and ends with a right estimation of God.

John also uses this order for the believer, while the unbeliever must firstly come to know God through Jesus Christ: "If someone says, "I love God," and hates his brother, he is a liar; for he who does not love his brother whom he has seen, how can he love God whom he has not seen? And this commandment we have from Him: that he who loves God must love his brother also." (1 John 4:20-21).

"Whoever believes that Jesus is the Christ is born of God, and everyone who loves Him who begot also loves him who is begotten of Him." (1 John 5:1).

Hurtful Criticism

If we are to be like Christ we must avoid being censorious: "Judge not, that you be not judged." This condemnation of others betrays the presence of hypocrisy in one's own life, a "plank" evidenced by a lack of love. The admonition against such judging, like the command to throw the first stone in John 8:7, redirects one's attention from the desire to correct or punish others to the need for personal repentance.

This doesn't mean that there is never the necessity to judge someone else. Indeed, the verses indicate that once a believer's own life is in order, he should remove the "speck" from his brother's eye, and Galatians 6:1 echoes the teaching that spiritual ones should aid in the restoration of those who have yielded to temptation. Furthermore, Matthew 7:16 give us the key to judgemental matters, saying, "You will know them by your fruits."

But a critical nature uncontrolled develops bigotry and is most unbecoming of a disciple of Jesus Christ. Our progress is to be made through prayer (verses 7-11) not through criticism, a point about which preachers and writers need also to be reminded. And if this is true in our relation to non-believers, how true it is concerning those linked with us in the Kingdom. David's heart smote him after he had cut off part of Saul's robe while they were in the cave, David's hiding-place; so should ours when we attack in others the works and position of which such robes speak. "But if you bite and devour one another, beware lest you be consumed by one another!" says Paul (Galatians 5:15).

"Put on therefore, as God's elect, holy and beloved, a heart of compassion, kindness, humility, meekness, longsuffering; forbearing one another, and forgiving each other, if any man have a complaint against any ..." (Colossians 3:12,13). The dual effect of this is outlined by Paul in Romans 14: "Therefore let us not judge one another anymore, but rather resolve this, not to put a stumbling block or a cause to fall in our brother's way ... For he who serves Christ in these things is acceptable to God and approved by men." (vv. 13,18).

Moral discrimination is necessary, but it must work in conjunction with love, and whoever converts a sinner from the error of his way saves a soul from death and covers a multitude of sins says James (James 5:20). Peter joins the thoughts: "above all things have fervent love for one another, for "love will cover a multitude of sins" (1 Peter 4:8).

Don't Cast Your Pearls Before Swine

The covering of sins, however, does not give permission to the unbelieving to treat precious things as paltry. Neither dogs, nor those so-called in scripture (compare the use of dogs and swine in 2 Peter 2:22) have an appreciation of holy things; nor do swine value either pearls or those who offer them. "But the natural man does not receive the things of the Spirit of God, for they are foolishness to him; nor can he know them, because they are spiritually discerned" (1 Corinthians 2:14). What the natural man can see is the very practical translation of Christ and His word through our lives as we treat others as we would be treated.

Ask, Seek, Knock

Christlikeness will demand prayer. Peter reminds us of Jesus' attitude throughout His life here, culminating in His crucifixion, in all of which He left us an example that we should follow His steps: reviled, yet unreviling, threatened, yet unthreatening (1 Peter 2:21-23). But prayer is more than taking one's frustrations to the Father. In Luke's fourteen references to Christ in prayer there is not one hint of this. Indeed, He calls on His Father to forgive the very ones crucifying Him; and instructs the disciples to pray, forgiving others, that their own debts might be forgiven. Consistent and continuing communication with the Father is the very essence of Christlikeness. With due regard to the Greek tenses, Wuest amplifies verses 17,18 this way:

"Keep on asking for something to be given and it will be given you. Keep on seeking, and you shall find. Keep on reverently knocking, and it shall be opened to you. For everyone who keeps on asking for something to be given, keeps on receiving. And he who keeps on seeking, keeps on finding. And to him who keeps on reverently knocking, it shall be opened. If we who are evil know how to give good gifts to our children, how much more does a heavenly Father know how to dispense good and unhurtful gifts?"

The culmination of this, the supreme Good Thing given to His own is the Holy Spirit (Luke 11:13). It is significant that the "Golden Rule" verse comes where it does after the parenthetical account of prayer. What is more, the word therefore indicates that the good we do for others is to be patterned on what we have received from God. Alford says: "... give that which is good for each, to each, not judging uncharitably on the one hand, nor casting pearls before swine on the other."

That is, we do for others not what suits us, making ourselves and our tastes the standards by which others must receive, but rather we do what we might have reason to believe they would like to have done unto them. And this standard of behaviour is not to be used with the idea of obtaining for ourselves our own desires from another. The exhortation is not seen to be manipulative, either in Matthew 7:12 or in Luke 6:31. It is a guide, not a goal for one's actions: "Let each of us please his neighbor for his good, leading to edification. For even Christ did not please Himself" (Romans 15:2-3).

Nevertheless, God is debtor to no man. When Job prayed for his three friends so that they would not be judged according to their folly, God not only answered his supplication on their behalf, but also restored to him what he had lost, and doubled the amount. As we fulfil the royal law, there will be blessings which also accrue to our account down here. Christlikeness brings with it present as well as future blessings: love, joy, peace, patience, kindness, goodness; faithfulness, gentleness, self-control. It brings the security and fellowship that such qualities imbue, and reciprocal blessings coming from others who will react in kind to the Christian treatment accorded them.

Anxiety

On a very practical note, much of the anxiety that unfortunately at times characterizes human behaviour will disappear as we observe the Lord's teaching. Worry changes nothing but the worrier, and that not for the better. It can't change yesterday nor tomorrow; its only power is to rob the present of much of its potential. Be not therefore anxious, for though each day has its share of evil, this very practical Sermon on the Mount speaks blessing upon blessing to all who will seek first His kingdom, and His righteousness. In our doing as we would have done to us, we both glorify God and bring many benefits to the lives of others and our own.

Matthew 7:12, through its fulfilment of the law and the prophets has a parallel with the love commandments of Matthew 22:36-40. Our correct horizontal relationships, man with man, as we live as sons of the kingdom, must flow out of that great vertical relationship of love we have with God through Jesus.

SUGGESTED PRAYER FOCUS

- That we may not miss out on God's good gifts simply by not asking for them.
- To trust that God as our Father has our best interests at heart and will meet our every need, not necessarily our every want.
- That we might take the initiative to "do unto others" rather than waiting for others to take the first step.

STUDY QUESTIONS

1. Why is Matthew 7:6 situated between two apparently unrelated passages?
2. What is meant by the 'pearls' of Matthew 7:6?
3. Without judging the other, how do we know when someone is a swine or a dog who we should not be 'casting our pearls' before?
4. In what contexts is Matthew 7:1 commonly used in the world today to justify an attitude of "live and let live"?
5. Are there ever occasions where judging a fellow human being is acceptable and indeed necessary?
6. Which Old Testament character was guilty of judging someone when he was actually the one who was guilty?
7. What do we learn about the matter of asking and knocking from Luke 11:5-8?
8. Read Matthew 7:7. Will God really give us everything we ask, or are there preconditions?
9. Why does Luke 11:9 say that God will give the Holy Spirit to those who ask, but the parallel passage in Matthew 7:11 says he will give 'good gifts'?
10. Name three key things that you would most like others to do for you or be to you. How can you apply the "Golden Rule" to these this week?

STUDY NOTES

11: CUT DOWN AND THROWN IN THE FIRE
(MATTHEW 7:13-20)

It's always been difficult to distinguish truth from error - or from the appearance of truth. It was difficult in the Lord's time when the uneducated common people had to rely on the teaching and interpretations of those in authority - the Pharisees and the chief priests. It was difficult in Old Testament times before that - with prophets prophesying messages which sometimes contradicted each other. And it's certainly difficult today with Christendom consisting of thousands of churches and denominations - with their own private doctrines and interpretations of scripture, and each convinced of their validity.

And so it is necessary in this world today to search for the truth. The present diversity is not of God; freedom to worship in a way which seems best to the individual is not God's way. God is looking for unity, not just a unity based on compromise, but a unity of those who adhere entirely to the truth that He has revealed. But how to recognize this today? The truth of God doesn't stand out as a beacon, apart and obvious, in this world so full of voices and beliefs. It will not be recognized by its popularity, for the seeker after God's truth will find himself as has always been the case, in the minority. "Few be they that find it," said Jesus of the narrow gate that leads to life (Matthew 7:14). And He instructed His hearers to strive to enter it (Luke 13:24), for the way is constricting; it requires submission to the will of God.

True and False Prophets

In Old Testament times, God provided His people Israel with the means of distinguishing a true prophet from a false prophet. In Deuteronomy 18:22 they were told that the test of a prophet who claimed to speak in the name of the Lord was whether what he had prophesied actually came to pass. Otherwise he had spoken "presumptuously." But a situation was also envisaged where a prophet might give a sign or wonder to draw away the people after other gods (Deuteronomy 13:1-5). That prophet was clearly false because what he said was contrary to the plain commandment of the Lord. He must be put to death. At the beginning of New Testament times, God provided evidence to substantiate those who were claiming to proclaim a new divine truth. They were given miraculous powers that others might believe (Hebrews 2:4). It was the test of the truth for that time. Jesus Himself said in John 5:36: "the very works that I do, bear witness of Me, that the Father has sent Me."

And so it was in Matthew chapter 7. To a multitude unable to discern for themselves false prophets and false teachers, He set out the cardinal rule: "you will know them by their fruits." Just as He took His illustration from nature, so the test of the truth was as foolproof and inevitable as the law of nature itself. Nature always reproduces after its own kind. Ten times that principle is repeated in the record of the creation in Genesis chapter 1. For example, it is impossible for an apple tree naturally to produce anything except apples. It is impossible for an animal such as a sheep to give birth naturally to any kind of an animal except a sheep. And, as Jesus pointed out in this chapter, it is impossible for a good tree to give corrupt fruit, and vice versa.

The test is the result that is produced everything "after its kind." In winter time, with only bare branches, trees may look alike. How can you tell one from the other? Not always from their branches, or necessarily even, with the coming of spring, by their leaves or their blossoms. Eventually the fruit itself will appear, and there will be no mistaking. The fruit is the real test. Similarly, how can you distinguish one person from another - whether he has the truth of God? Not by his appearance, or even by his words - all that can be deceiving. The true evidence of the character and faith of the man is what he does: is it in accord with Scripture?

James recognizes this in his epistle. In chapter 2, verse 20 he says that "faith without works is dead." From verse 14 to 26 he explains clearly, not that works are a substitute for faith, but that they are the evidence of that faith. This evidence serves an important purpose. It's quite possible to be a believer in Jesus Christ today secretly. But we are instructed to let others know, not to hide our light under a bushel. And how will they know? By our fruit - our works. When the Sanhedrin saw the boldness of the apostles Peter and John, they marvelled, and acknowledged that they had been with Jesus (Acts 4:13). John the Baptist demanded that those who were coming out to him to be baptized should "bring forth fruits ... worthy of repentance" (Luke 3:8). Even God Himself said (in Malachi 3:10), "And try Me now in this," says the Lord of hosts, "If I will not open for you the windows of heaven and pour out for you such blessing that there will not be room enough to receive it." In these cases and others, it was important that there be the evidence.

Let's make sure at this juncture that what we are saying is not misunderstood. Works are not a substitute for faith; they do not give salvation. The scripture is very clear on this: "For by grace you have been saved through faith, and that not of yourselves; it is the gift of God, not of works, lest anyone should boast." (Ephesians 2:8,9). But, notice Paul's next verse: "we are His workmanship, created in Christ Jesus for good works ..." Again, works are not the cause, but the product, the evidence of what has taken place. Just as the apples don't make an apple tree, but merely show that it's an apple tree, so our works don't make us believers, but just reveal what we do believe.

Our good works are important to God; not for salvation, but for proof of our faith and for service. We have been created in Christ Jesus that we might do them! It is significant to note that what God judges in every dispensation of men is their works. It's true of believers in Jesus today; at the Judgement-seat of Christ, it's the believer's works that will be evaluated - for reward or loss (2 Corinthians 5:10). His eternal salvation is already secure. So also it is in the future judgement of the nations in Matthew 25; it's their works on which they will be judged - as the proof of their faith. Similarly, at the great white throne judgement at the end-time (Revelation 20:12), the dead will be judged "out of the things which were written in the books, according to their works."

The Fruit of Faith

What then are the works, the fruit, that faith should produce - the fruit which is the evidence to others of the truth of God within us? Certainly not success in winning converts, or the popularity of our cause. Firstly, it is that we shall be doing the will of God, as Jesus went on to say in Matthew 7:21. And then, as He told His disciples, this is how the world would know them: "By this all will know that you are My disciples, if you have love for one another" (John 13:35). Surely this is the greatest work of all, the truest evidence of the genuine work of God in a human heart, the unselfishness of love. This is the fruit of human character changed by God Himself. It can't be manufactured; it can't be imitated, because the fruit is the product of what's inside.

1 John 3:9-10 (NIV) says: "Whoever has been born of God does not sin, for His seed remains in him; and he cannot sin, because he has been born of God. In this the children of God and the children of the devil are manifest." We see then that the test of the tree is its fruit; the test of the person is his works. How often has it been said, in one form or another, "what you are

speaks so loudly, I can't hear what you're saying." Or "what you do tells me what you really believe." It's a serious thing to realize that the test of the validity to others of what we say and what we preach is our works, our actions. How much effort is expended in personally testifying to the gospel of Jesus and in teaching His disciples, and yet our influence in this is only as great as the extent to which our own lives are consistent with it. Our hearers are examining the fruit.

Each of us who professes to have the truth of God in his heart must first apply this test to himself. The apostle Paul told the saints in the Church of God in Corinth, "Examine yourselves as to whether you are in the faith. Test yourselves. Do you not know yourselves, that Jesus Christ is in you?" (2 Corinthians 13:5). If we have been privileged with divine insight into God's truth, how are others to be able to see that? By the fruit. By the genuine love, and the consistency of our actions. Do we live Christ as well as preach Christ? Do we show the truth as well as teach the truth? That's how others will tell and how we'll be effective in reaching them. And if not, can we expect the truth to remain with us? For, as Jesus said, "Every tree that does not bear good fruit is cut down and thrown into the fire." (Matthew 7:19) May the world be able to see clearly and distinguish in us the truth of God, and know us by our fruits.

<u>SUGGESTED PRAYER FOCUS</u>

- That many will find the narrow way.
- That God will reveal his Will that we may walk in it.
- That we will always build on rock and not sand.

STUDY QUESTIONS

1. Who or what is the narrow gate of Matthew 7:13?

2. Does Matthew 7:14 imply that only a minority of the human race will ultimately be saved?

3. What makes the way that leads to life so difficult (Matthew 7:14)?

4. Does Matthew 7:19 imply that a lack of good works means we can be eternally lost?

5. How do we know what the Father's will is, so that we can do it (Matthew 7:21)?

6. What is the 'rock' that the wise man built on?

7. What is the 'sand' that the foolish man built on?

8. What does Matthew 7:29 mean when it says that, unlike the scribes, Jesus taught with authority? Didn't the scribes have the authority to teach?

STUDY NOTES

12: FIRST THINGS FIRST

There's a great deal of helpful instruction in a consideration of what Jesus placed first in His teaching. Jesus said in the 'sermon on the mount', "... if you bring your gift to the altar, and there remember that your brother has something against you, leave your gift there before the altar, and go your way. First be reconciled to your brother, and then come and offer your gift." (Matthew 5:23-24).

This is in keeping with that word in the Proverbs: "To do righteousness and justice is more acceptable to the Lord than sacrifice" (Proverbs 21:3). The ways of the offerer and his heart condition were more important with the Lord than the value and quality of the gift. To defraud or oppress one's neighbour, or trespass against him, and yet to come before God with a gift, was quite contrary to His mind. God laid the greatest stress on the seed of Abraham keeping the way of the LORD and doing justice and judgement (Genesis 18:19), and so He told Abraham of His prospective visit to Sodom to make inquisition concerning injustice and sin of all kinds which were being committed there.

Even with a righteous man like Lot sitting administering judgement in the gate of Sodom, there was no improvement of its moral condition. Who should ascend to the hill of the LORD with his gift, there to stand in His holy place? The answer is: "He who has clean hands and a pure heart, who has not lifted up his soul to an idol, nor sworn deceitfully" (Psalm 24:4). Again David said: "I will wash my hands in innocence; so I will go about Your altar, O Lord" (Psalm 26:6). The order is first reconciliation, then offering, both in Old and New Testaments.

Seek Ye First

One of the Lord's most precious promises relative to all the material needs of His people is that contained in Matthew 6:33: "But seek first the kingdom of God and His righteousness, and all these things shall be added to you." The weight of Jesus' promise rests on the word first. To give the kingdom of God second, third, or fourth place, or no place at all, as is true in the case, alas, of many of God's children, is to go against our own well-being in this life.

Where did Jesus put this matter in the prayer which He taught His disciples? He placed it first. "Your kingdom come, Your will be done, on earth as it is in heaven," comes before "Give us this day our daily bread" (Matthew 6:10-11). Isn't the matter of daily bread and how it is to be got the first consideration with many? Is it so with us? Jesus' injunction is to seek the kingdom first. Pray for it first. Then bread and clothing, and all needful things that may be classified under such headings, will be added. There can be no failure of His promise. If we see to His things, He will see to ours. "Has His mercy ceased forever? His promise failed forevermore? (Psalm 77:8). Never! "Has God forgotten to be gracious?" (Psalm 77:9). No, never! His covenant promise is "I will never leave you nor forsake you" (Hebrews 13:5).

Let Me First

In contrast to putting first things first, we are told (just after the conclusion of the 'sermon on the mount'), "Then another of His disciples said to Him, "Lord, let me first go and bury my father. But Jesus said to him, "Follow Me, and let the dead bury their own dead" (Matthew 8:21). There are times when men in the service of their king and country are granted compassionate leave, but there are other times when such cannot be allowed. In the Lord's things there may also be circumstances when the call and claims of Jesus are such that they over-ride those of father and mother, of wife and children, and of all earthly responsibilities. The martyrs had to consider which was first, Jesus or their friends, and so also have we.

Jesus' words were sometimes scathing. He could not bear hypocrisy. When speaking of brethren judging and condemning their brethren, He said, "Judge not, that you be not judged. For with what judgment you judge, you will be judged; and with the measure you use, it will be measured back to you. And why do you look at the speck in your brother's eye, but do not consider the plank in your own eye? Or how can you say to your brother, 'Let me remove the speck from your eye'; and look, a plank is in your own eye? Hypocrite! First remove the plank from your own eye, and then you will see clearly to remove the speck from your brother's eye" (Matthew 7:1-5).

Haven't we seen it in life's experiences, that harsh, unmerciful men, when they had power, imposed on weaker brethren the full forty stripes, without taking the Roman discount of one off, little thinking that the Lord's words were on their track and would overtake them one day? How painful it has been to see men drink the full measure of the cup they held to the lips of others! Haven't there been others whose interest in spiritual things seemed to be to look for and point out faults in others? The Lord detected this tendency in His time, and told such persons to get rid first of the plank in their own eye, before they sought to help their brother with his speck. But a righteous man, who is as severe upon himself, or even more so, than he is on others, will kiss the rod of his correction. David said, "Let the righteous strike me; It shall be a kindness. And let him rebuke me; it shall be as excellent oil; let my head not refuse it." (Psalm 141:5).

But who can bear mere carnal fault-finding, when such a fault-finder is the brother with the plank in his eye? The bee and the blue-bottle when they cross a field are attracted to different objects, the bee by the flower with its beauty and scent, the blue-bottle by the corrupting carcase or other foul-smelling object. What are we attracted by in fellow-believers, to see Christ (in such measure as He may be seen) in such, or to hunt for their carnal defects or weaknesses?

Men in all ages have tried to reach to higher heights of spirituality by setting aside the plain commandments of God. This was Satan's deception which he successfully plied on Eve, when he assured her that in the day they ate of the forbidden fruit she and her husband would be as God. The lure was tempting and she took it. Paul saw the approaching evil of men forbidding to marry and commanding to abstain from meats, doctrines of demons, the lure being the same, that men would get up higher by means of the purification of the flesh, and would reach a plane of spiritual life unattainable by men who followed the course God had outlined for men on earth.

The Pharisees and scribes, too, by their traditional teaching of the washing of hands, by which they sought purity of mind and body by what went into men, and by their teaching that men should give all their earnings to God (no thought was to be given to the first commandment with promise, regarding the honour to be paid to a man's father and mother (Matthew 15:1-14) made void the word of God. But it was all of the same evil origin, that man was to get up higher by disobedience.

First Learn …

Paul's words are clear and corrective, "But if any widow has children or grandchildren, let them first learn to show piety at home and to repay their parents; for this is good and acceptable before God" (1 Timothy 5:4). The proverbial saying that "charity begins at home" expresses the truth. Paul adds the very powerful words, "But if anyone does not provide for his own, and especially for those of his household, he has denied the faith and is worse than an unbeliever" (verse 8). Let us attend to what comes first, then we can attend to other things as they come in their order, remembering that "first" does not mean "all." The order of responsibility is (1) the home, (2) the church, (3) the world. Each has claims upon us.

SUGGESTED PRAYER FOCUS

- For the determination to sort out any issues with our brothers and sisters first before we approach God.
- For help to seek God's Kingdom first.
- For grace to see the best in our brothers and sisters in Christ, and not the worst.
- For the discipline to praise and honour God in our prayers first, before we ask.
- For preservation from a Pharasaical, legalistic mindset.

STUDY QUESTIONS

1. Are rules always a bad thing? (see 2 Timothy 2:5)
2. Are traditions always a bad thing? (see 1 Corinthians 11:2, 2 Thessalonians 2:15, 2 Thessalonians 3:6)
3. 1 Timothy 5:4 uses a word which is not commonly used today – piety. What does it mean, and how can this be shown at home in particular?
4. What does praying for daily bread indicate about the frequency of our prayers?
5. The disciple of Matthew 8:21 wanted permission to bury a dead family member, but this was denied. Yet 1 Timothy 5:4 says we should provide for our own. How do we reconcile this apparent inconsistency?
6. Why might our responsibility to our family come first, before the church?

13: THE TEACHER WITH UNIQUE AUTHORITY

The Sermon on the Mount ends with a brief but vitally important epilogue. "And when Jesus finished these sayings, the crowds were astonished at His teaching, for He taught them as one who had authority, and not as their scribes" (Matthew 7:28-29). (Quotations in this chapter are generally taken from the Revised Standard Version.)

The Teacher
The Sermon began with the Lord Jesus withdrawing to teach His disciples, but evidently the crowd followed to hear more from this outstanding person. At the end they were therefore astonished or, more literally, shocked. For the person they knew as Jesus of Nazareth, and who had already shown evidence of having special powers to heal the sick (Matthew 4:23), could also teach in a way they had never heard before, although He had not been trained in the schools of the rabbis (religious leaders). The

Jewish people had been diligently taught in the Law of God, which was given through Moses. The scribes (teachers) had not only sought to explain the meaning of the Law, but they had expanded it with their own Oral Law, which contained a multitude of detailed interpretations. None of these teachers could claim any authority of their own, but could only seek to be faithful to their traditions.

The Old Testament prophets had spoken as they were directed by God, which is evident by their usual preface, "Thus says the Lord" (e.g. Isaiah 43:14, Jeremiah 2:2). The fundamental difference of this new Teacher was His unique authority, which is shown by His frequent use of personal pronouns. "I" is used 18 times in this section, generally in the form "I say to you" (Matthew 5:18); He also refers to "these words of Mine" (Matthew 7:24). He was the only one who could speak this way, because He was the only begotten Son of God, who was sent by God the Father to be the Saviour of the world. He did not explicitly state His deity at this time, although this truth emerged in discussion with the Jews. Peter could later exclaim, "You are the Christ, the Son of the living God" (Matthew 16:16), but it was not until the ascension that the disclosure was made to all: "All authority in heaven and on earth has been given to Me" (Matthew 28:18).

The theme was developed by other new Testament writers: "In the past God spoke to our forefathers through the prophets at many times and in various ways, but in these last days He has spoken to us by His Son, whom He appointed heir of all things, and through whom He made the universe" (Hebrews 1:1, 2

NIV). Here was the supreme Teacher of all time, who was God and who came to make Him known (John 1). Unlike other teachers He was more important than even His message, and His call was first, "Follow Me."

His Mission

This Teacher made it clear that He had come for a specific purpose; as He said, "Think not that I have come to abolish the law and the prophets; I have come ... to fulfil them" (Matthew 5:17). His teaching was not therefore something in isolation, nor was it opposed to the Law in any way, as some of His hearers apparently suspected, but it represented the culmination of the prophetic witness. He intended to carry out everything that was required to the smallest detail, which is described as a jot or iota, in such a way as to manifest in His life the glory of God (John 1:14). He magnified the Law and made it glorious (Isaiah 42:21).

The ceremonial regulations would be suspended, and the sacrifices would be superseded by His one great sacrifice, but the cardinal principles of justice, mercy and faith would be enhanced (Matthew 23:23). If His listeners were confused He would demonstrate to them that their teachers were at fault in their interpretation of the Law. For they had forgotten the real intention of the Law, which was to provide a standard of conduct for Israel to maintain the special relationship which they enjoyed under the Old Covenant. The scribes had drawn up hundreds of regulations, which they sought to impress by their compliance and outward observance, so seeking to justify themselves before God. They even went so far as to grade by merit the commandments: some were called greater and others lesser, hence the reference to the least of the commandments (Matthew 5:19). All this was far removed from the essential requirement to love the Lord your God with all your heart, and your neighbour as yourself (Matthew 22:37-39), which will continue for all time. God was looking for a standard of righteousness and for inward obedience, which had been foretold by Jeremiah: "I will put My law within them, and I will write it upon their hearts; and I will be their God, and they shall be My people. And ... they shall all know Me" (Jeremiah 31:33-34). So the kingdom or kingly reign of God was at hand, and it was not surprising that the religious leaders were angered as He challenged their teachings.

His Standards

Since the people's understanding of the Law was unsatisfactory, and needed both correcting and extending, He demonstrated the standards that God required by six antitheses, where the contrast is brought out by "But I say to you" (Matthew 5:22 etc.):

1. Matthew 5:21-26. The sixth commandment prohibited murder, but He extended this to include anger, that is a brooding revenge that harboured thoughts of murder, and He included with this the contemptuous insult, which impugns the character. As murder will kill a person, so also these aspects of hatred will destroy a person. The necessary corrective is first to seek reconciliation, which should be done before offering any sacrifices.

2. Matthew 5:27-30. The seventh commandment prohibited adultery, but He extended this to include the sin of lust, which is the desire to commit adultery. His remedy for this is very

dramatic, that is, to pluck out the eye and to cut off the hand. He was not advocating self-mutilation, as some have since attempted, in vain. He was taking up the Jewish saying that the eye is the medium through which temptation comes, and the hand is the instrument through which sin is carried out. The implication is that a limited life is better than a depraved one.

3. Matthew 5:31-32. Divorce was permitted under the Law, and the rabbis had been much occupied in interpreting Deuteronomy 24:1-4, and in particular defining the circumstances of "if she finds no favour in his eyes." But He was not interested in their various attitudes for acceptable grounds for divorce. He was only interested in stressing the permanence of marriage.

4. Matthew 5:33-37. The taking of oaths is described in Deuteronomy 23:21-22. Although oaths may be required in special circumstances, they had come to be used frivolously, and also profanely to impress others. But He required that God's name should not be used in oaths, even indirectly, such as swearing by heaven, which is the throne of God. Rather He says, "Do not swear at all."

5. Matthew 5:38-42. Since retaliation tended to be excessive, the Law limited it to the extent of the aggression. But His requirement was to stop any retaliation, even for an extreme insult, as is implied by striking the right cheek. To take it further, help must be given to all who require it.

6. Matthew 5:43-48. The Law required the people to love their neighbours, but it contained no reference to hating your enemy, which was a later addition. The scribes considered their neighbours to be fellow Jews; but Gentiles, who were considered to be evil persons, were hated. He required that they should be like God, and love all men.

These illustrations all show in a practical way how Jesus required a higher standard from His disciples than was required by the Jewish teachers. This was summed up in the following: "You, therefore, must be perfect, as your heavenly Father is perfect" (Matthew 5:48). This standard could only be attained by the grace of God in those who have known the new birth. It was no wonder that when the full realization of these hard sayings dawned on many of His disciples they no longer followed (John 6:60). His sayings were sometimes difficult to understand, and all were difficult apart from divine grace to put into practice.

His Method

The large crowds that followed Jesus showed the effect of both His personality and His outstanding ability to communicate with His audience, whoever they were. His sayings contain many different figures of speech, which give vitality to the message, whereas the Jewish teachers were dull and tedious. The following examples, taken from the Sermon on the Mount, show the wide range that He used.

(a) Simile - "Even Solomon in all his glory was not arrayed like one of these" (Matthew 6:29).

(b) Metaphor - "The eye is the lamp of the body" (Matthew 6:22).

(c) Proverb - "For where your treasure is, there will your heart be also" (Matthew 6:21).

(d) Dramatization - "If your right eye causes you to sin, pluck it out and throw it away" (Matthew 5:29).

(e) Hyperbole - "Why do you see the speck that is in your brother's eye, but do not notice the log which is in your own eye?" (Matthew 7:3).

(f) Extension - "If you then, who are evil, know how to give good gifts to your children, how much more will your Father who is in heaven give good things to those who ask him!" (Matthew 7:11).

(g) Questions – "Are grapes gathered from thorns, or figs from thistles?" (Matthew 7:16).

(h) Poetic form - "Ask, and it will be given to you; Seek, and you will find; Knock, and it will be opened to you" (Matthew 7:7).

He also used puns, which are not obvious in our translations, and parables, which were based on happenings in everyday life. The purpose of these illustrations was to impress the minds of the people by relating his teaching to their own environment. This subject has not received sufficient attention, and all teachers could profitably study more in depth how He taught.

The Response

In the conclusion (Matthew 7:21-27), Jesus gave a very serious warning to His audience. Unlike ordinary teachers, whose sayings can be accepted or rejected with only limited consequences, His sayings demand a full active response; He solemnly directed them to "that day." This is the time that the prophets had looked forward to, when evil-doers will be banished, and when God's will must prevail. In that day He will be the Judge for, "the Father ... has given all judgement to the Son" (John 5:22).

False teachers and prophets who have deceived others will be exposed, for no one can deceive Him. Their claim to have done mighty works in His name, and even to have called Him "Lord" will not be accepted. All who have not willingly responded to His teaching will then be sentenced as evil-doers, who will find no place in the future glorious kingdom. This subject is further developed in Matthew 24 and 25 where the disciples are reassured of the final triumph over evil.

The warning is illustrated by a simple parable about two builders. Anyone who hears the words of Jesus, and does nothing in response, is like the foolish man who erected his house directly on the sand. All was well until the time when the rain, floods and wind beat on the house; as a result the house collapsed completely, for there was nothing to support the structure (Matthew 7:27). But those who heard the words of Jesus and obeyed were like the wise builder who first dug down until he found rock, and on this he built his house, which was able to survive the impact of the elements, although perhaps the wind beat even more strongly on this house. The foundation on the rock made all the difference. Elsewhere we are told, "For no other foundation can anyone lay than that which is laid, which is Jesus Christ" (1 Corinthians 3:11). It should be emphasized that this parable is not teaching salvation by works, but the need for a sure foundation. His authority was thus firmly established with His disciples, who were left in no doubt that God was working powerfully among His people, and that Jesus would lead them to know God in a real way. He can still do that today!

SUGGESTED PRAYER FOCUS

- For help to be doers of the Word and not hearers only (James 1:22).
- That the word of the Lord will grow mightily and prevail (Acts 19:10) run swiftly and is glorified (2 Thessalonians 3:1).
- That the word of Christ will dwell in us richly in all wisdom (Colossians 3:16).
- That we might faithfully sound forth the word of the Lord in every place (1 Thessalonians 1:8).

STUDY QUESTIONS

1. Read 2 Timothy 4:3. Has this day now arrived? Explain your answer.
2. Is it possible that Jesus Christ could simply be a great philosopher and teacher and yet not be God's Son and the Saviour of the World?
3. Read 2 Peter 2:1. How can we recognize false teachers today? (e.g. see 1 John 2:21-22, 1 John 4:1-3).
4. After completing this study, what part(s) of the teaching of the Sermon on the Mount is the Holy Spirit impressing on your heart as needing further attention? What next?

STUDY NOTES

MORE TITLES FROM HAYES PRESS

I f you've enjoyed reading this book, you may be interested in our other paperback titles:

Hayes Press Series
- The Finger Of Prophecy
- The Parable Of The Tabernacle
- A Study in Prophetic Principles
- Exploring Issues Of Life
- The Call Of Christ: Living Life To The Full
- Down In My Heart To Stay: Experiencing God's Joy
- Back To Basics
- Where Is God's House Today?
- What Have We To Give?
- Looking Into The Heart Of God – A Study of David

Many of these titles are also available in e-book format on our website.

Search For Truth Series

- Healthy Churches: God's Bible Blueprint For Growth
- Hope For Humanity: God's Fix For A Broken World
- The Supremacy of Christ
- Once Saved, Always Saved? The Reality of Eternal Security
- Fencepost Turtles: People Placed By God
- Jesus: What Does The Bible Really Say?
- The Tabernacle: God's House of Shadows
- A Legacy of Kings: Israel's Chequered History
- Minor Prophets – Major Issues
- Tribes and Tribulations – Israel's Predicted Personalities
- One People For God (Omnibus)
- Kings, Tribes and Prophets (Omnibus)
- God – His Glory, His Building, His Son (Omnibus)

ABOUT HAYES PRESS

Hayes Press (www.hayespress.org) is a registered charity in the United Kingdom, whose primary mission is to disseminate the Word of God, primarily through literature. It is one of the largest distributors of gospel tracts and leaflets in the UK, with over 100 titles.

Hayes Press also publishes Plus Eagles Wings, a fun and educational Bible magazine for children, six times a year and Golden Bells, a popular daily Bible reading calendar in wall or desk formats. Also available are over 100 Bibles in many different versions, shapes and sizes, Christmas cards, Christian jewellery, Eikos Bible Art, Bible text posters and much more!

As well as its retail operations, Hayes Press is also a full-service publisher and is happy to provide a competitive quote for all your printing needs.